JOB HUNTING IN EDUCATION

An Insider's Guide

Herbert F. Pandiscio

Published in partnership with the
American Association of School Administrators

ScarecrowEducation
Lanham, Maryland • Toronto • Oxford
2004

Published in partnership with the
American Association of School Administrators

Published in the United States of America
by ScarecrowEducation
An imprint of The Rowman & Littlefield Publishing Group, Inc.
4501 Forbes Boulevard, Suite 200, Lanham, Maryland 20706
www.scarecroweducation.com

PO Box 317
Oxford
OX2 9RU, UK

British Library Cataloguing in Publication Information Available

Library of Congress Cataloging-in-Publication Data
Pandiscio, Herbert F. (Herbert Frederick), 1931–
 Job hunting in education : an insider's guide to success / Herbert F.
Pandiscio.
  p. cm.
 "Published in partnership with the American Association of School
Administrators."
 ISBN 1-57886-116-0 (pbk. : alk. paper)
 1. Teachers—Employment—United States. 2. Teaching—Vocational
guidance—United States. 3. Job hunting—United States. I. American
Association of School Administrators. II. Title
LB1780 .P36 2004
370'.23'73—dc22

2003026501

∞™ The paper used in this publication meets the minimum requirements of
American National Standard for Information Sciences—Permanence of Paper
for Printed Library Materials, ANSI/NISO Z39.48-1992.
Manufactured in the United States of America.

To my wife and colleague,
Ruth Pandiscio

CONTENTS

ACKNOWLEDGMENTS

For more than ten years in her role as consultant, Ruth Pandiscio—my search firm colleague who also happens to be my wife of many years—has provided the moral and logistical support without which the firm could not have experienced its many successes. For the candidates, she was always there, giving them the benefit of the doubt while treating them as friends. The burden of reading thousands of their applications and resumes fell to her. Most of them will never know of her thoughtfulness in promoting their careers. And I thank her for the many hours she spent editing the material in this guide.

I also thank Russ Farnen of Avon, Connecticut, who gave so generously of his time to edit this guide and to provide ideas for the reorganization of some of the materials.

PROLOGUE

It had been a long and trying winter for the tribe. The days were short and darkness settled early in the village. The winds were fierce, the snow deep, and food in short supply. The children no longer smiled and the women resisted their men. The dances lacked the excitement of old. Festivities brought no joy to young and old alike. The young braves were restless and the older warriors kept to themselves. The council, comprised of the elders, had not met for some weeks for fear that any discussion would not be purposeful. And the traditions of the tribe made it impossible for the young to be heard. A blanket of silence settled over the village. There seemed to be no end to the discontent.

Although the tribe was strong and respected among the other tribes, the spirit had gone out of its people. There was whispering among the young braves and the warriors that the time had come for the chief to pass his authority to another. This was difficult for them to acknowledge because the chief was loved and respected. He had done much to make the tribe the strongest and most renowned in the entire area. But many in the village worried that the chief was no longer strong enough to ward off the ambitions of other tribes and that a new, rival chief would not respect the people.

The elders of the tribe who had survived the wars of the past also knew the time had come for their chief to step aside. No one had the heart to share with him the feelings of the tribe because they knew how much he had given to his people. Of all the chiefs in all the land, he had been the most fearsome warrior of all, yet he possessed the wisdom of the gods. He had brought peace to the land and until now had secured the future of the tribe. Because of this, the braves and warriors and elders kept their silence through this terrible winter.

Spring came in all its glory, and the land regained its beauty. The worries of the winter disappeared like the burning of the morning fog. The problems faded in the minds of all, except for one. The chief, being the wisest of them all, knew the time had come for another to lead his people. He wanted to believe that the leadership of the tribe could pass to one of the braves but they were so young! Could a young brave command the respect of others? And then there were his warriors, those who fought so often to protect the village. No, he did not question the courage of his warriors but he was not certain that any had shown the spirit needed to lead. The elders on the council had served the people well yet he pondered whether they were too old and tired to envision the future. He worried that none of the elders was prepared to succeed him. Yet he also questioned if he had taken the time to judge his warriors, braves, and elders fairly. It troubled him that perhaps he had overlooked leadership potential in all of them. His concerns grew daily because the time was near when he would need to make a decision.

When the time was right, he assembled his elders and announced his plans to name a new chief. The custom of the tribe was that a chief names his successor. Because of the deep respect the elders had for him, they allowed the chief's wife and eldest son to join the council meeting to express their thoughts about the chief's successor.

Once the council had assembled, the chief asked his wife, son, and then each member in turn to describe the qualities of the leader who should succeed him. His wife was definite in her comments that the new chief should be like her husband for he was the bravest warrior of all and the other tribes would soon challenge a new chief. Without a warrior in charge, the village would soon fall to another tribe. She was clear in her opinion that her husband had a responsibility to protect the village through his choice of a successor.

His son spoke next and demanded that he be designated the new chief for he knew what it would take to be a leader, having observed his father all these years. "Leadership is not learned, it is in your blood! I am the eldest son of the chief and the only true heir and leader." And, in turn, each elder on the council spoke and made known his wish. "I want a great warrior, stronger than all the others" spoke the first. "I want a man of wisdom who can lead by example," said the next. "We need a healer, one who gives the people hope," commented the oldest. From the youngest of the elders came, "Without a hunter, our tribe will die." Another claimed, "There are vast lands beyond the horizon that are yet to be explored. Only a man of vision can lead us there." Yet another spoke, "We must return to the values of the old days when we had the courage to protect all that was of value to our ancestors. The future is now." "I wish a leader who values each of us and promotes equality," said yet another. And the last concluded, "We must have a chief who sees all nations as one, lest we fight to the death of all of us."

And so it went around the council table. Each member expressed an opinion, yet none agreed with the others. The chief reflected on what each had said and then announced that on this same day in the following week he would assemble all of the young braves, the experienced warriors of the tribe, all of the elders, and his son. At that time he would begin his selection process. The elders were told to spread the word that all were to assemble in the village at sunrise of the designated day.

Then he told the elders, his wife, and son that he would speak with the chiefs of other tribes and urge them to send their most outstanding braves and warriors to the assembly. Dumbfounded, the elders questioned why he would invite warriors from other tribes to this meeting. His wife and son stared at husband and father in disbelief. How could he even think of passing over his own son for the son of another? Blood is blood! Family is family!

The chief sought their silence and told them that it was his responsibility to appoint the best leader for his nation. It was vital that other tribes send their very best to be considered for the position of chief. Whether the leader comes from within or without is not the issue, he told them. "The goal is to have a leader who can preserve the best of the past, adjust to the current conditions, and secure the future of the tribe."

Word quickly spread throughout the village that a new chief was to be named, that braves and warriors from other tribes were invited to the assembly, and that one of them might be named chief. Some thought looking outside the tribe was a brilliant move because they believed that a leader from another tribe could bring new ideas to the elderly council members. Others were troubled by the thought that no braves or warriors in the tribe were considered worthy to lead. Confusion reigned throughout the village.

Without waiting to be told, each brave and warrior of this and the other tribes began to plan how he could outmaneuver the others. Each tried to anticipate what the chief would be seeking in his successor. Each was planning on how he could outdistance himself from all of the others. Each knew that he must present himself in a chiefly manner; all knew that the chief had the final word in choosing his successor. None knew exactly what the chief was looking for, but each had to decide if he would try to anticipate what the chief wanted and pretend to be something he was not, or to be true to himself and present his ideas for better or worse. Each of them faced a different dilemma.

On the designated day, hundreds of young braves hoped to prove themselves worthy of leadership while experienced warriors assumed one of them would be appointed. They assembled at sunrise on the hill overlooking the village. While the elders knew that none among the council members would be selected, they joined the assembly for this historic occasion. The son, mounted on the finest pony that the tribe possessed, pranced in front of all. Each was prepared to risk his life if need be to prove his courage. Each was dressed in battle clothes. Braves and warriors from all the other tribes clustered together, suspicious of the chief because they questioned if he would give an outsider an opportunity to prove he had the leadership skills needed to succeed him. Their concerns were somewhat diffused because the chief was known in the entire nation not only for his courage but also for his integrity.

The chief looked out at the gathering and felt awe at the scene. He, too, like those in the assembly, faced a dilemma. He asked himself, "How do I identify among this multitude the leader of my tribe? This is the strongest tribe in the entire nation and it must remain so. It is true I am tired but I have given my people a sense of purpose, the resolve to be stronger than all others, the wisdom to honor the traditions of the past, the insight to seek new answers to the questions of survival and growth. I have also honored our ancestors while looking to the future.

Now, I worry that the wrong choice will destroy all that the village people have acquired through their sacrifices. Whoever leads our tribe must respect the knowledge of the elders, the courage of the braves, the contributions of our women and families, and protect and enrich the lives of our children. He must view our history as a way to frame the future. He must understand that true leadership results from relying upon the work of others. While strength of body is required, it is through wise leadership that our people will best survive and prosper."

On this day began the chief's quest of identifying who among the hundreds of available candidates would lead his people. He had never been called upon to make such a momentous decision in his lifetime. But now the moment was upon him. None of the braves, the warriors, or his son, the logical heir, had ever been at such a momentous juncture in their lives. No other tribe had ever looked outside its own for a leader. While the chief knew that what he had done so far was right, he had yet to frame the standards of comparison so as to be fair both to the village people and to those who aspired to be chief.

Quietly, he said to himself, "When the sun sets this day, there must be a new chief for the tribe. Just as I hunted for food to feed the village, I hunt now for my successor to ensure the future of the tribe."

INTRODUCTION

My wife, Ruth, and I often play golf while on vacation. Being a twosome, we usually get teamed up with another twosome. On this particular day, the other twosome was comprised of two young, strong-looking Norwegian guys in their twenties who were in this country on vacation. Decent golfers ourselves, we nevertheless wondered how we would keep up with them. As it happened, they were pretty bad golfers. The bright side was that they both spoke excellent English and were good company. We were quickly at ease with one another, on a first-name basis, and engaged in a typical conversation between those of different nationalities. Because I was, at the time, working on a foreign language program proposal for a school district, I was interested in how and when they learned to speak English.

From the outset, both expressed surprise at how far and straight Ruth was hitting the ball from the tee box, something they did not expect from a middle-aged woman. She shared with them the fact that although I was not a low handicap golfer, I had developed the knack of diagnosing her golf game, was patient, and was able to give clear and easily understood feedback. I mentioned to Christian and Larz that the ability to diagnose problems and find solutions is a talent that most teachers and administrators develop during their careers. It is practiced every day in every classroom where there is an outstanding teacher and in every schoolhouse where there is a talented administrator. Find yourself an outstanding school system and most likely you will discover a superintendent with first-class diagnostic skills. Consequently, Ruth learned to play golf, not from a low handicapper, but from a diagnostician. I mention that I provided clear and easily understood feedback to Ruth because many of the lessons that we took from golf professionals, for the most part, left us more bewildered than proficient. Their feedback was much too technical and complicated.

We played several holes, each worse than the other for the guys. My game was fair and Ruth's was strong. Christian was preparing to tee off when he stopped during his practice swing and called over to me, "Herb, would you mind showing me how you taught Ruth to drive the ball?" Correcting the problem was easy enough because the answer to his problem was simple, but one he could not see in himself. He could have hit another hundred balls that afternoon but, without help, his problem would not only have remained, it would have worsened. His problem was not unlike that of candidates involved in the job hunt. A simple, uncorrected mistake can become a high-handicap problem.

I was reminded of the encounter with Christian when I started on this book. When I began my search for that first administrative position, I never thought to ask someone to show me how to "hit the job-hunt ball." I hit away, time and again, and each time reinforced the same errors. Christian had no embarrassment about asking for help, in part because I was a stranger and in part because he was secure enough in himself to look to someone else for assistance. In observing Ruth's game, he had firsthand evidence of how simple feedback, clearly stated, can make a difference. He took advantage of the situation and profited by it. But I have seen both experienced and inexperienced educators make the same recruiting errors repeatedly and never seek help. As is so often the case with golf instruction, what you receive for job-search advice leaves you more confused than enlightened. This guide is about getting you to hit the job-hunt ball long and straight from the outset. My suggestions to Christian turned out successfully for him—just as they are likely to be for you.

If you study this guide carefully and compare what you have been doing with what I recommend you do, based on the experiences of other candidates, you will develop a level of confidence and skill that should get you into the winner's circle. Each anecdote in this book is just that—a short story based on an actual experience.

Everything noted is associated with a candidate or employer with whom I have worked. As expected, I have changed the names or descriptions of candidates, occasionally the gender, states, locales, and the size and demographics of districts, but the basic information presented is as I recorded or remembered it. None of these minor changes alters the validity of the advice offered.

It is possible that you may be involved in a job search that is tainted from the outset, and you will stand no chance to be appointed. Many candidates, including myself, have been in just such a situation. It is not unusual for an employer, consultant, superintendent, or board to have a favorite candidate and merely go through the motions of a search to give it a veneer of legitimacy. For example, you may see job postings that appear on a time frame so short that there is no reasonable way for you to apply in time. This gives the appearance of a job already filled. Job descriptions may be written to favor certain candidates and to exclude others. On the other hand, a district may require a doctorate, knowing that no inside candidate possesses one. Occasionally—and although illegal—gender, age, race, nationality, and religion will play some role in a selection process. Educational and professional pedigree may come into play. For example, the college you attended and the district in which you worked may be of importance to the hiring district. The makeup of the group that screens applications and the profile of the interviewers can skew results. If you are in any of these situations, my advice is to forget it and move along. Nothing you say or do will alter the ethics of those who do not play fair. Taking legal action can be an expensive and painful experience. Thankfully, in the vast majority of cases, the search process is legitimate.

If you fail to be selected for the job you seek in a district that has a good record of engaging in a comprehensive and open job-search process, it most likely will be due to what you did poorly, what you failed to do that was expected, or it could have been a case of not having the required background and experience. But if you made it to the first interview and got no further, it is probably because of how you presented yourself. You failed to use the interviewing opportunity to make your case. Blaming the process will only impede your making required changes in your approach. The sooner you change, the better your chance for success.

WHO WILL PROFIT FROM THIS GUIDE?

The stories and suggestions in this guide chronicle the efforts of hundreds of candidates with whom the author worked as they engaged in a job hunt. As you work your way through this guide, you will read the stories of experienced administrators who failed to understand the competition they faced for new positions and who were so often passed by. You will also read about wonderful but inexperienced candidates who stumbled and failed in their efforts for lack of skillful guidance. And you will also read the many success stories and the hundreds of positive suggestions that flow from those stories. It is for these reasons that this guide will be of value to those seeking positions in education either as a teacher or administrator.

This guide is also written for those responsible for hiring teachers and administrators. The success of candidates depends greatly upon the quality of the search process the consultant and employer establish. So often we are led to believe that it is only the candidates who need to be schooled in effective job-hunting techniques when, in fact, their efforts are only as good as the job-hunt process in which they become engaged. I have had experience with employers who failed to create a positive environment in which candidates could fairly compete for a position. As a result of the ineptness of interviewers, I have seen highly qualified candidates passed over while interviewers chose less-qualified candidates for a job. There are many suggestions in this guide, some direct and some through implication, for those who have the responsibility to create an effective and fair recruiting program.

The following groups will profit from this guide:

1. Those seeking a first-time administrative position in education
2. Practicing educational administrators below the rank of superintendent who wish to move to a central office or superintendent position

3. Experienced superintendents who seek a more challenging position in public education or a move to a related position in the private or nonprofit sectors

4. Teachers who plan to pursue different teaching positions, either in or out of their current districts

5. Undergraduate and graduate education majors who have much to learn prior to securing their first job

6. College and university educators who wish to make a career change into elementary and secondary education or to nonprofit organizations

7. Governing board members who have a major say as to who is hired in their districts and who, through their group and individual behavior, create the organizational and employment culture of the district

8. Human relations personnel in both the public and private sectors who need to create appropriate protocols for use in establishing an effective and fair job-search process

9. Those in a "people" business who wish to prepare for a job search and who need to discover effective methods to research a position, create a "perfect" set of job documents, and learn how to use interviews to their advantage.

10. Those in private industry who may be considering a career move into education and who need to understand the culture of education and the code language of the profession

11. Anyone who can profit from an insider's perspective on what does and does not work effectively in a job hunt

Now, on to the subject of how to avoid failure and practice success.

❶

AVOID THE ACT OF FAILURE, PRACTICE THE ART OF SUCCESS

It was May and I had just earned a master's degree in secondary education. One month later I was married; three months after that, I started my first teaching job at an outstanding regional high school in suburban Mass-achusetts. The school system was recognized nationally as a leading district and was the recipient of a vast amount of funding for pilot programs from both the federal government and regional colleges and universities. An outstanding superintendent supported by a highly qualified faculty and administrative team led the district. I felt privileged to be hired for my first teaching assignment in such a positive setting. Within a year, due to the illness and subsequent retirement of my department head, I was promoted to that position. It was not long before I knew that what I earned as a teacher fell far short of what my family would need to live comfortably. Like so many other teachers of that era, I looked forward to the salary and benefits that went with a full-time administrative position.

ADVICE, PROFESSIONAL TO NOVICE

Having begun my doctoral studies while in that first teaching position, I believed I was prepared to begin my hunt for that first administrative position. How wrong I was! My principal at that time was a straight-talking educator with a very direct style, but there was also a sense of mutual admiration between him and his staff. He was a person to be trusted. Knowing that I aspired to become an administrator, he took me aside one day and told me that his current assistant principal had no intention of retiring anytime soon and the best way to kickstart my administrative career was to look outside the system. I really did not want to hear that. In retrospect, it was some of the best advice I ever received, and it is advice I often give to others in my role as consultant.

He also told me that the best way to stymie a career was to stand in line and wait for someone to leave or die! As it happened, his assistant principal remained for many years; by the time he retired, I had held three administrative positions. For me the cliché "Up and out" was really "Out and up."

THE QUEST BEGINS

Following my principal's advice, I began my quest for an administrative position outside the district. With only three years in the classroom, two of them as department chair, I knew it would not be easy to acquire that first administrative position, but I was still confident I could do so. The graduate school I attended had an ineffective job placement service and provided no training on how to secure a new position. I was on my own with no administrative job-hunting experience. Fortunately, I had learned how to collect accurate background information while being trained to work in military intelligence prior to entering education. Extensive work in the writing of succinct and focused reports as part of that training was a benefit to me when I needed to create a cover letter and resume. As a result, acquiring a first-level interview was simple enough. But, once there, I ran into a blank wall.

The mistakes I made are documented throughout this guide along with the mistakes made by hundreds of other professionals with whom I worked for over thirty-five years. It was not until my nineteenth interview that I was offered my first administrative position. When that first offer came, we had one small child and my wife was expecting another. Both of us were physically and emotionally close to our parents and families and knew we would miss them greatly if we moved any distance—

but I wanted that first administrative position, even if it meant moving out of state. My wife was supportive of the move. (The importance of spousal support is addressed in chapter 7, "Please, No Notes from Mother.")

My new district was rural and located in upstate New York. Considering the fabulous seacoast community where we were living, upper New York State could just as well have been another planet. The student body was far tougher than what I had known, and the district was very different from the one in which I was working.

It was a very lonely time for all of us. Although a difficult move, it was also a successful one primarily because of the effective mentoring that two great principals provided me, one where I had taught and one in my new district. Interestingly, they were very different in their management styles, but both were effective at mentoring teachers and administrators. My former principal told me "do not wait until someone retires or dies; just go for that first administrative position." His message was "get out to go up."

My new principal, a humanist through and through, taught me that high school students needed the support and caring that we were professionally responsible to provide. He modeled every day what he expected from me and from his staff. With his support and blessing, I was back in my home state with my own principal position within a year. Administrative advances came quickly after that, and I became a superintendent within six years, at the age of thirty-six.

SECOND PLACE IS LAST PLACE

I learned many lessons from those early failures, failures you need not experience. I had, without wanting to do so, learned the art of failure. And knowing what I know today, I want to believe I could have acquired that first administrative position with one attempt if I had taken the time to learn how to recruit for a new job and if there had been someone to "help me drive the job-seeking ball long and straight." This guide is about helping you find success in your job hunt. Many of the lessons recited here were learned by virtue of mistakes others have made. Every lesson described has behind it a candidate or client with whom I have worked. This guide is short on theory and long on experience. You can rest assured that the mistakes described herein have been made by many others and will continue to be made. The goal of this book is to minimize your chances of making these mistakes.

When I am working with aspiring administrators, they will often share with me their most recent job-search experiences wherein they placed second and felt really good about it. My response is always the same: no matter how positive you may feel about coming in second, it is no better than being last! I know—I was there eighteen times!

During the twenty-five years I spent as a public school superintendent, I personally interviewed close to 2,500 candidates for teacher and administrator positions. Of those 2,500, I hired approximately 500. During my next ten years as an educational search consultant, I interviewed another 1,000 or so candidates for high-level administrative positions. Of this latter group, 100 to 125 were ultimately hired. In addition, I have monitored hundreds of interviews that my employer clients conducted.

These numbers do not include the thousands of applications received from aspiring teachers and administrators in my former school system and by my firm that were judged unacceptable because of a poor presentation of materials. Outstanding candidates are not always outstanding at preparing cover letters and resumes or in building an attractive career paper trail. Some of the most inept candidates are the most experienced administrators and teachers. They are either too proud to take advice or have been out of the job market so long that they do not comprehend the level of competition they face. Often, they do not receive quality feedback from colleagues or from potential employers. What feedback they do get is usually vague, noncommittal, and of little value.

PROVOCATIVE QUESTIONS

You have to ask yourself, why is it that some candidates are hired and others are continually passed over? What is the secret of gaining employment when you have the professional credentials that often are superior to those of the candidate selected? What mistakes did you make early in the application process that resulted in your not being moved along? Why is it that after only a few minutes into an interview you know you are out of the running? Or why, after what you thought was a great interview, were you not offered the position? What words or phrases turned interviewers off? What interviewing strategies did you fail to employ? How well prepared were you for the interview? At what point in the interview did you lose your advantage? What caused interviewers to fail to recognize your talents? What mannerisms did you display that embarrassed you or the interviewers? What really went wrong, and why has no one told you? What impressions did you create with your opening comments and concluding remarks?

Having worked with thousands of candidates over a thirty-five year period, I know how discouraging it is for those not selected for a position. I have seen the best and the worst of candidate interviews and job-search activities. And, over these many years, I have documented the application and interview process as a way of helping those who have not been successful in a job search. Many candidates make serious errors well before they are out of the gate. From the beginning, the odds were against them. For many of those who were granted an initial interview, they continued to make mistakes throughout the process. Unable to afford private job coaching, they never learned why they failed in their job quests. This guide is the best, most available, and probably the least expensive advice they may get, starting with a warning to be careful where they decide to work, the topic of chapter 2, "The Career Ladder."

2

THE CAREER LADDER

This guide concentrates on efforts to assist you to identify, compete for, and acquire a new position. It covers the essential elements of a search and, if you accept suggestions that apply to you, the chances are excellent that you will reach the winner's circle.

DO YOUR HOMEWORK

However, be careful that you "don't rush in where angels fear to tread." There is an old saying, "the faster you run, the quicker you fall behind."

Before you actually apply for a position, you must engage in a comprehensive analysis of the position, the district, its governance, the quality of the staff, and those who will supervise your work. If you are competing for the position of superintendent, you must examine the track record and behavior patterns of the board and its leadership. Your failure to conduct comprehensive research can have profound and sometimes devastating consequences. If you are applying for a building-level administrative position, you need to investigate the superintendent in terms of how he works with staff. Is your new boss a person who holds trials or one who mentors colleagues? In the same vein, a teacher needs to know how the principal operates with staff. (See chapter 8, "Holmes and Watson, Front and Center," for more information on conducting your investigation into the school district and its leaders.)

There are times when you should not apply for a position because the probability of your success is not high. There are districts and positions where you will fail, not because you are you, but because the conditions that exist do not provide the platform to be successful. The question is, how does one determine the potential for success or failure? In real estate, the mantra is "location, location, and location." In any job search, whether in the public or private sector, the mantra is "research, research, and research." I must emphasize the importance of gathering good data. Without quality information, you are at a disadvantage. You must accept the fact that there are other candidates who are collecting data in order to make sound decisions. For example, if other outstanding candidates declined offers from the district, you need to determine why they did so. Do they know something you do not know?

As an interim superintendent, I have worked in a district where a significant number of potential candidates refused to apply because of the negative reputation of the governing board. The word had gone out that this was not a favorable environment in which to work. It does not, however, mean that someone would not be successful; simply put, the leader's philosophy had better be in tune with that of the governing board. Therefore, when offered a position, be certain that you do not allow your vanity and financial needs to get in the way of reason. Learn how to say no if you are uncertain about the logic of accepting a position.

How you approach the decision to apply for a position and decide whether or not to accept one (if offered) should be a function of two factors. The first is to determine where you are in terms of your professional career ladder. The second factor has to do with how badly you need a job. Having held the positions of teacher, department head, coach, assistant principal, principal, assistant superintendent, superintendent, search consultant, and eight interim superintendent positions in a variety of cities and suburbs, I believe my perspective on career moves is an accurate one.

The movements described below are typical of career ladder changes. However, there will always be exceptions and variations. Professional moves are not always linear nor are they always upward.

FROM "SOMEWHERE" TO TEACHER

The first step in the educational career ladder begins with that first appointment as a teacher. Job hunting for your first position will be a challenge. Because of the many factors that impact those seeking their first teaching position, this step on the career ladder is covered in more detail in chapter 16, "Special Thoughts for Aspiring Teachers."

FROM TEACHER TO ENTRY-LEVEL ADMINISTRATIVE POSITION

Moving from a teacher position to an entry-level administrative position (e.g., department head) that does not carry direct line responsibilities is one of the easiest moves to make. It usually means shifting from a classroom teacher position to department head or a similar type of nonsupervisory job. Most often, you are early in your career, you have expertise in a subject or function area, and the move will usually carry an added stipend, increased salary, and some additional degree of professional prestige. The risk of failure is minimal since you will usually be cast as a support to other teachers and not necessarily as an evaluator, regardless of years of experience. But even if the evaluation of others is included in the job responsibilities, your expertise in the area will almost guarantee your success primarily because someone higher up in the hierarchy will ultimately make the decision whether one of the employees you supervise is recommended for nonrenewal or termination. You may be required to provide data that is used in the decision, but others will make the final call. These entry-level positions are some of the most sought after in education. When you seek these jobs, it is usually because you decide to make a professional move and not because you were forced out of your current position. The advantages of such a move are the same whether you are early in your career or somewhere along the career ladder continuum.

FROM ENTRY-LEVEL POSITION TO ASSISTANT PRINCIPAL

Moving from a teacher or department head type of position to that of an assistant principal position is somewhat more difficult and somewhat

riskier. An assistant principal is in a line position where final decisions must
be made in those areas of responsibility that have been delegated by the
principal. In a line position, you will have to take unpopular stands. At the
secondary level, assistant principal positions usually include dealing with
student discipline or special education—almost always challenging assignments. Often, you may not be popular with students who think you are
unfair, while teachers may see you as being too soft. In addition, you will
invariably have a number of teachers to supervise and evaluate; you will either be making decisions that impact livelihoods or will be contributing to
evaluations in a major way that impacts others. Unlike the input given by a
department chairman, the decision of an assistant principal usually carries
more weight. In either case, you begin the slow march up the hierarchy
and begin to antagonize others. It is a far different situation from that of
department head or teacher. For perhaps the first time in your career, you
will begin to cultivate adversaries.

An added risk in making the move to an assistant principal position
has to do with where you make the move. If it is an internal promotion,
the chances are you competed both with insiders and outsiders. If with
outsiders alone, your promotion is without concern. When you compete
with other insiders, there is always the slight chance that there may be
envy on the part of colleagues who did not get the appointment.

If you are appointed to an assistant principal position in another
school system wherein you received the nod over an inside candidate
who remains in the district, often in the same school, you need to exert
caution. Those who had favored an inside candidate will closely monitor
your work; some will hope you fail and others may help you do so!

Finally, and importantly, your new position will initiate the slow but
steady change in your lifestyle. All too often, aspiring administrators do
not have a clear understanding of the price to be paid for increased
salary and prestige. Given the shortage of outstanding administrators,
school districts, state departments of education, and higher education
institutions are constantly encouraging outstanding teachers to move
into administration. Be thoughtful about these enticements since you
may get what you wished for.

The greatest change that takes place in a move from the position of
classroom teacher or department head to assistant principal will be the
number of evenings you will work and the lengthened day, almost every

day. Additionally, you will be required to work on some weekends, during vacations, and at other times that are not convenient either for you or your family. Although outstanding teachers often work long days, it is not every day, and the decision to work is one they make and is not one that is imposed upon them. As assistant principal, you have no choice. I find it troubling that so little attention is given to this aspect of the job change. One hopes that those who enter administration will have no regrets as the years slip by and as they recognize the changes that are taking place in their lifestyles.

FROM ASSISTANT PRINCIPAL TO PRINCIPAL

The next logical move on the career ladder is from assistant principal to principal. It is at this stage that the concerns raised about the assistant principal position are magnified several times over. Other than the position of superintendent of schools, this is the most demanding job in education. And, contrary to public perception, the job of elementary principals is now more demanding, in my experience, than that of middle school or high school principals. Over the years, there has been a shift in this regard. The change has to do with the involvement of parents of elementary school children. While most elementary school principals and teachers will discreetly refer to such parents as "involved," in many cases they are outright "intrusive" and unreasonably demanding. Few principals can withstand the power and demands of elementary school parents. In addition, most governing boards do not have the will to defy these parents, especially since many governing board members came up through the ranks of the PTO or PTA. Individually or as a group, parents usually get what they want. In most schools in this country, elementary school principals have no assistant principal, and they find it almost impossible to create a free minute during very long days to think or reflect. This is not to say that secondary-level administrators do not have tough jobs because they do, especially in terms of the many night and weekend commitments. But the pressure from parents is not of the same intensity and frequency as is experienced at the elementary level.

However, whether you are an elementary school or secondary school principal, you will be responsible for making difficult and controversial decisions. On one hand, you are the academic leader; on the other hand, you are one of the major decision makers in terms of the future livelihood of your staff members. Controversy waits on every corner, many of your teachers are Monday morning quarterbacks, and parents judge you on "what have you done for my kid today?"

In addition to the increased job responsibilities, the next greatest change will occur in the continuing imposition on your time and changing lifestyle. There will be more evenings out, more weekends committed to work, with beepers, cell phones, voice mail, and e-mail to tie you to your job no matter where you are or what day of the week or hour of the day it is. As principal, you may not see your superintendent on a daily basis, but with beepers, e-mail, voice mail, and the like, you have no place to hide! You are on duty 24/7.

The risk factor associated with the move from assistant principal to principal is significant. The performance of students and teachers will be your direct responsibility. Underperforming schools usually have underperforming leaders. Underperforming leaders often become unemployed leaders. You need to think clearly about this move and make certain that you locate to a district where success is obtainable and that those who work for you and those for whom you work share the same or similar visions for the school.

FROM PRINCIPAL TO CENTRAL OFFICE

On the table of organization, between the position of principal and that of superintendent of schools, there are numerous positions with districtwide responsibilities. Educators in these positions usually work out of the central office and report either to the superintendent or assistant superintendent. At a minimum, most districts will have professionals for business, pupil personnel services (including special education), and curriculum. In larger districts you will find deputy superintendents, or similar positions, plus subject area coordinators. Depending upon the organization, those in these positions may or may not have the evaluation of others as part of their responsibilities. Regardless of whether or not they carry evaluation responsibilities, these positions are generally considered attractive ones with minimal professional risk involved, especially for those in the positions of assistant superintendent or deputy superintendent. Each position has the security blanket of knowing that the superintendent will eventually make a final decision on controversial matters. Workdays and work year are generally well defined. Evening and weekend work is limited. Unlike principals who always have some-one afoot, central office employees have loose schedules that afford them the opportunity to step away from their work during the day for a breather. The salary is higher, benefits oftentimes more generous than those received by principals, and they are usually immune from having to deal directly with parents and students. The one exception is that of special education supervisor, by whatever name. That position remains somewhat of a crucible. All in all, however, these are good jobs to ac-quire. It is from this cadre of central office personnel that most super-intendent candidates will be identified.

Central office positions are mentioned here because they are often a place of refuge for principals who wish to back away from line responsi-bilities. Many principals are qualified for most central office positions. For that reason, with the exception of a special education administrator and occasionally the business manager, all central office jobs usually have a more than ample supply of qualified recruits.

FROM PRINCIPAL AND CENTRAL OFFICE TO SUPERINTENDENT

Principals are being appointed to superintendent positions at an in-creasing pace because of the shortage of qualified candidates. This final step in the career ladder for elementary and secondary education ad-ministrators is the most challenging of all. The sheer workload of the su-perintendent can be overwhelming, the infringement on personal and family time is monumental, and the actual risk of job loss is a constant cloud. Nevertheless, in spite of the negative aspects of this move, there are those who wish to cap their career by being a superintendent of schools.

Having made the moves up the career ladder in a linear fashion from teacher to superintendent, I personally experienced the increased re-sponsibilities and stress levels with each movement and lived through the different lifestyle changes. The most valuable advice that I can offer to those aspiring to reach the top of any administrative hierarchy is that you must carefully consider what value you place on a quality lifestyle. Each movement upward demands that you pay a price. This final move to the top of the hierarchy is the costliest of all. A comprehensive look at the risks associated with this professional move is covered in chapter 17, "Life at the Top: The Universe of Superintendents."

The following chapter, "Communication Tools," describes in detail the earliest preparations for a successful search. While the "tools" appear to be simple in nature, your failure to provide for them can have profound consequences.

3

COMMUNICATION TOOLS

A job search often gets off to a shaky start because of a failure to pay attention to communication tools. It has been said that great events often turn on small hinges. Although your communication tools may appear to be a small hinge in a complex search process, they could make or break your search efforts. Communication tools include simple but important items such as the answering machine, business voice mail, fax, home telephone, vacation phone numbers, cell phone, and e-mail. Unless you have programmed your equipment properly and educated and informed those who tend to the equipment and who answer on your behalf, you may never get your search off the ground. We have initiated thousands of phone calls, faxes, and e-mails over a ten-year period. It is fair to say that we have experienced about every traditional and nontraditional response one can imagine. There are candidates to whom second calls have not been placed because of their inappropriate responses or non-responses to our first calls.

The following explanation of the communication tools required on a job hunt also provides examples of serious shortcomings we have experienced.

HOME ANSWERING MACHINE

First, you need one! It is not unusual to have candidates engage in a job search and not provide us with a convenient way to reach them by phone. It is inconceivable to me that a professional searching for a position would not have an answering machine, but it happens. We generally do not place a second call if a candidate does not have an answering machine.

It is strongly suggested that you personally create the answering machine message and not rely on others to do so. Over the years we have heard tapes by teenage girls who speak so rapidly you are uncertain you have reached the correct number, and by high school boys who view this as an opportunity to practice mumbling. We have heard messages made in many foreign languages, in song, in poetry, in jest, and with religious overtones and messages. We have heard messages that would be insulting to any caller. The most memorable "nonmessage" is one that was made by an incoherent three-year-old daughter of one of our candidates. A simple message is still the best. How about trying, "You have reached (insert area code and number). Please leave a message and phone number, and I will return your call as soon as possible."

BUSINESS PHONE AND VOICE MAIL

It is important that you inform your consultant or potential employer if it is appropriate to contact you at a business number. If so, then make certain that you can be reached. Voice mail has become so impersonal and technical that it is often difficult, if not impossible, to reach a candidate. We worked with an experienced and outstanding superintendent who wanted us to contact him using only his voice mail at work. It turned out that the way the equipment was programmed, it was not possible to reach him! Simply impossible! When I finally connected with him at his home phone number, I suggested that he try to call himself to see if he could get through. Remarkably, he could not reach himself!

I strongly suggest that if you want others to use your business voice mail, you should try calling your own voice mail to check for the effectiveness of the message that greets the caller. I did just that while I was engaged in an interim superintendent position and decided to check on the district's voice mail system. It was the month of August when I tried reaching the office after regular business hours. The phone message on the system was a holiday welcome from the previous December. You need to ask yourself how a consultant or future employer will react to that voice-mail message.

Many administrators, especially superintendents, have their voice mail directed to private secretaries rather than to themselves, a system that, in my opinion, defies logic. I really have no interest in talking to a candidate's secretary. Under such a system, you cannot leave a message directly with the superintendent. If, however, you are committed to this foolishness, you need to let your consultant or potential employer know if messages dealing with future employment are to be left with your secretary either personally or on his voice mail. For 95 percent of the superintendent offices we call, the voice-mail menu is programmed such that the mailbox for the superintendent is the last item on the menu, requiring the caller to listen to all other mailbox numbers before reaching the superintendent's office. When a superintendent lists her voice mail last on the menu, it simply reinforces the hierarchical nature of the operation. It says, "Don't call or bother me!" Interestingly enough, building principals with whom I have worked usually had their mailbox number listed first.

HOME PHONE

Once you have the answering machine issue settled, you need to address the matter of phone calls that are answered by you or others. Let us start with you. If the call is from a consultant or employer, you need to be businesslike. Listen to what is said, accept the instructions, and bring closure without entering into a conversation about unrelated matters. It is a business call, and you should treat it as such. If you do not understand something that has been said, ask for clarification immediately since you may have a difficult time getting back to the caller once you disconnect. If the purpose of the call is to make an appointment with you, be certain to write down the time, date, and location and then repeat it to validate the information. It is appropriate to ask if you are expected to bring any documents to the meeting. If not, then do not bring any materials with you except for a 3 × 5 inch index card and a pen.

It is important that any person who has access to your home phone be informed that important calls related to a job search may be coming through for you. Each person should be told to record the caller's name and phone number, and to inform the caller that his call will be relayed to you as soon as possible. If the caller provides other information, then the receiver should repeat what has been stated to validate it for accuracy. We have had many cases where messages have not gotten through to the candidate when left with teenagers. The same problem is encountered when we reach homes with household help or nannies who have a very limited knowledge of English. I recall working with the chair of a governing board in a very complex search. Leaving messages at her home phone was questionable because her household help had a poor understanding of English. In this case, I relied almost entirely on reaching the chair by cell phone. It is up to you to make certain that calls get through. You may not receive a second one.

FAX MACHINE

Given the economical price of a fax machine, it is inexcusable not to have one at home during a job search. Although it may not be used frequently, when needed it is a valuable tool. Most often it is required when documents need to be transferred quickly pending receipt of hard copies. As a consulting firm, we accept signed fax applications to assist candidates meeting deadlines although we require a hard copy with original signature. It is not necessary to have a dedicated line for your fax machine, but if it is a dual-purpose machine, you must program it so that it is capable of receiving messages at any time. This is particularly important when the candidate is one or more time zones away from the consultant or employer. Members of your family or others with access to the fax should be alerted to the fact that important messages for you may be arriving. You should designate a location in your home where incoming fax messages are placed. If you are using a fax machine at work, once again, you need to authorize the sender to use it; otherwise, employees in your office may inadvertently gain knowledge of your job search.

VACATION CONTACTS

Consultants and employers work on their schedules, not yours. What may be your vacation period is not necessarily theirs. If you have applied for a position and know that you will be on vacation, whether in the country or out, you need to make it convenient for the consultant or employer to contact you unless you choose otherwise. If you are traveling out of the country, you should consider a phone service that allows you to be reached. They also need to know the dates you will be away and not available for an interview. More than one candidate has been eliminated because she was not available during her vacation period.

I worked with a candidate who was the front-runner for a superintendent position, one that he was well qualified to hold and one in which he had expressed a strong interest. He was on vacation when he received the call to confirm his final interview. At the time, he was on the West Coast and the interview was on the East Coast. The schedule was such that he could have easily arranged a round-trip flight, but decided he didn't want to spend approximately $500 for an airline ticket and thus passed up a great opportunity. Because he knew beforehand that the schedule for the final interview would occur while he was on vacation, he should have decided before he left town not to accept an interview and so informed the consultant. Instead, he chose to make the decision while on vacation and at the last minute, inconveniencing both the potential employer and consultant.

By his scheduling an interview and then canceling, he denied another colleague the opportunity to compete. Because it was a last-minute cancellation, we did not have time to reach and schedule another candidate. We did not represent this candidate again.

CELL PHONES

Cell phones have eased considerably the problems associated with contacting candidates. We strongly suggest that you have a cell phone with messaging capability. Keep in mind that all of the precautions associated with fax, phone, and voice-mail issues also need to be addressed when you program messages on the cell phone. You need to educate everyone who has access to your cell phone in the same manner you would with a regular phone. Because of reception and battery problems with cell phones, you need to have a backup number available.

The best example of the value of a cell phone was experienced while working with a candidate from the West Coast who had applied for a position on the East Coast. We communicated solely by cell phone. No matter where he was, I was able to contact him. With messaging capability, he never missed a message left for him. I rank him number one in terms of staying in contact with us during a search. This same candidate is also a perfect example of a "call back," a situation where he competed for and did not receive one superintendent appointment, but because of his outstanding interview I called him back to compete for another. He received the appointment in the second district. The importance of a call back is explained in detail in chapter 18, "Reflections."

E-MAIL

This is a great way to transmit attachments of hard copies of materials needed quickly. However, material sent is not always received. Thus, you should still mail hard copies. Because most candidates have e-mail availability both at work and home, it must be made clear which address is to be used. As a consultant, the most common worry is that someone who is not authorized to receive information about a candidate's job search activity will, either purposely or inadvertently, intercept e-mail messages sent to a work address. Most of our administrative candidates have secretaries who also have access to their e-mail messages. It is the responsibility of the candidate to provide the consultant and employer with appropriate information as to where messages should be sent. It is unsettling to the consultant to leave a job-hunt message on the voice mail and e-mail of a secretary.

The best example of the effective use of e-mail was in working with a rural/suburban district. Because of the difficulty of the governing board getting together for formal meetings, the only way to reach all of them was by e-mail. This in itself is not unusual, but in this case a condition of conducting the search was that I had to use e-mail for all communications and for the distribution of materials. The members did not want

either hard copies or faxed copies of any documents except for the actual applications. With the governing board established as an e-mail
group, e-mail became an efficient communication method both for the
members and for me.

Now, let us consider the issue of self-disclosure and owning up to your
hidden past!

4

YOUR HIDDEN PAST

When conducting preliminary interviews with applicants for any position, I always conclude the session with the question: "Is there anything in your personal or professional background, which if it were to become known publicly, would bring disgrace to you, and embarrassment to me and to the employer?" Each candidate will have a different take on what "disgrace" and "embarrassment" mean, but all understand the significance of the question.

A candidate may believe that an incident in his background is an impediment to a job search while in my opinion it may not be. Therefore, I encourage the candidate to continue in the process until we determine the seriousness of the incident. Another candidate may disclose an issue that requires considerable discussion to determine what impact it would have on a job search if it were to become known publicly. A few have purposely misled me in the hope I would not learn of a serious incident in their past.

The lesson one should learn is to have trust that your consultant is able to provide a sounding board for you to discuss what may become an issue. Failure to be honest with your consultant will most likely result in a severance of the relationship. If a consultant is not involved, then you need to work with a trusted friend or colleague for a third-party opinion.

You can assume that when you reach the final stages of a job search and are considered competitive enough to be selected, the employer and consultant will conduct background checks. The most important topics pursued during a background check will focus on evidence of success and indicators of problems.

EVIDENCE OF SUCCESS

Your ability to provide quality service in your area of specialization is the most important aspect of your candidacy. If you do not have the requisite professional credentials and experiences, you minimize your chance of advancing in the process. Depending upon the position for which you applied, the professional background check may take one of several different paths.

For nonadministrative positions, the background check is most often conducted by telephone. While most employers will contact some or all of the references provided on the application, others will go beyond that and call additional contacts who have knowledge of your work or who have some basis to make valid judgments about your professional work. Employers place great value on your ability to work successfully with other professionals. Many candidates have mastered subject matter but have failed to develop the high-level interpersonal skills needed to be successful.

Do not assume that the references you listed will be the only ones contacted. The rule of thumb when it comes to background checks is that consultants and employers will go wherever the trail takes them to get at the truth. They cannot afford to overlook an issue that could undermine their choice of candidate.

If you are applying for an administrative position, it is a certainty that, at a minimum, a site visit will be conducted in your current school district. Districts that fail to conduct a thorough site visit often live to regret it. Within the last two years, a governing board in a Northeast school district failed to conduct a site visit before making a superintendent appointment. Within a year, the new leader was in serious trouble because of his style. If a site visit had been conducted in his former district, there is little question that his leadership style would have surfaced within a few hours of meeting with his former employers. I am aware of this case because I happened to be in this superintendent's district on other business and the stories of his leadership style were legend, offered even without asking. His new district forced him out before the end of his second year.

In some cases, I have advised an employer to visit both the current site and the previous site to validate a candidate's work history. Generally, if a consultant is involved, she will provide a list of the persons to be contacted during the site visit to an employer. In some cases, the employer will also have additional names for the list. The employee is also encouraged to suggest the names of those in the school or community who have specific knowledge about significant successes that he wants known to the visiting site team. At some point, a complete list of references will be developed, and a site visit schedule will be constructed.

As a former superintendent and consultant, there are three areas I focus on when conducting a background investigation, whether it is a telephone check or a site visit. The areas of focus carry differing weights depending upon the position to be filled. However, all three areas are investigated.

First, I want concrete evidence that you were successful at every position you held, no matter how small the successes or how minor the position. It is the history of success that is important. Where you are headed in the profession will reflect in large measure where you have been. If there was an occasion where an experience was out of character for you, I must have a full understanding why this mismatch occurred.

Second, I want evidence that you have worked successfully with other professionals at every level of the organization, including members of the staff who are in support and service positions. I am reminded of a superintendent who was about to hire an assistant principal for his high school. The front-running candidate at that time was a high school classroom teacher in an adjoining town. The superintendent decided that he would make the site visit to the high school where the teacher was employed. First, he made a call to the superintendent in the district to acquire his opinion about the candidate. Satisfied with that conversation, he decided to conduct the site visit alone.

The feedback was that he spent better than half a day in the school, and the only individuals he spoke with were secretaries, custodians, cafeteria workers, and students. He obviously was interested in how his potential assistant principal would work with those whose opinions we often fail to consider but who make school systems operate at top efficiency. He was also interested in what students thought of this teacher and how they would view her as an assistant principal. Positive relationships form the basis for success in education. Highly honed interpersonal skills are an intelligence I expect to identify in all leaders. The superintendent learned that his candidate possessed both qualities.

Third, I want evidence that throughout your career you were always one of the first to volunteer to take on those extra projects as a way of standing out from the crowd. Anyone can do what is expected; few do more than they need to. As a consultant or employer, I need to have a way to cut you out from the crowd. One way for me to know this is to determine if you distinguished yourself as a volunteer for school projects. How willingly did you step up when the principal or superintendent asked for assistance on a project?

If you have not distinguished yourself in your current position, it is time you did so. You will not be able to make up tomorrow what you failed to do today. Professional couch potatoes are not in high demand!

INDICATORS OF PROBLEMS

Criminal Record

When you apply for a new position, you most likely will be given a questionnaire inquiring if you have been arrested or convicted or if you have criminal proceedings pending against you. You must answer the questions honestly since most districts will conduct a formal criminal record check once you are employed. If you lied on the application, the district most likely will have the legal right to dismiss you out of hand. Most questionnaires will ask for your maiden name and other aliases that you have used. Whatever the questions, give truthful answers.

If you have a criminal record, it is best to ask the consultant or employer if it would disqualify you from contention. For example, it is not unusual for candidates of a certain age to have attended college during the '60s and '70s when drugs were commonly used on and off campus.

Some may have been arrested and convicted for drug use or for campus disruptions. It is also not uncommon to have candidates who had been arrested for driving while under the influence of liquor. This can be a serious issue depending upon how active anti-drinking groups are in the region. Only the potential employer can determine if the public exposure of an arrest and conviction would create a major issue in the district.

I worked with an outstanding superintendent who was driven from his position because of a drug possession arrest that took place when he was eighteen years old, some twenty years in his past! A brilliant career was stopped dead in its tracks. He was employed in a large metropolitan district where dirty politics included destroying a reputation, if necessary. I had worked with this candidate on a federal grant many years earlier when he was an elementary school principal. I knew the quality service he had provided, and I respected his talents. After the incident mentioned above forced him out of his position, he applied for another position in a district where the board was conducting its own search, and I was hired to conduct background checks on twelve semifinalists. He was one of the twelve. We discussed his drug arrest and how the public disclosure of it had adversely impacted his tenure in another district. To paraphrase the question I asked of him, "What will your reaction be if you are hired and the issue of the drug arrest surfaces once again? Given the toll it took on you the first time, will you be able to manage the negative press?" He thought about it for a few days and then made the decision that he could not hold up emotionally if he had to go through a public debate a second time. He therefore decided to withdraw.

At the other end of the administrative continuum, I worked with a former assistant high school principal who was forced from his position because of a "driving while intoxicated" arrest. He left the state in which he had been arrested and carved out a successful career in education in another state, attaining the position of assistant superintendent in a large suburban district. Some years later, he wanted to return to New England and applied through me for a superintendent position in a town that was within twenty miles of the district in which he had been arrested when he was an assistant principal. It was also within the same circulation area of the major metropolitan newspaper that carried the original story. During our interview he talked freely about the drinking issue in response to the question, "Is there anything in your personal or professional background, which if were to become known publicly, would bring disgrace to you, and embarrassment to me or to the employer?" He went on to share with me that his moving out of state after his arrest was a good decision. He had been a teacher in the general area and still had a support group. They made it possible for him to start over, an opportunity many do not get.

At the time of my interview with him, it was obvious he was professionally qualified for the superintendent position he had applied for— but the issue of the drinking incident and the arrest remained. My question to him was, "If the drunk driving charge of many years ago is made public, can you stand the adverse and controversial publicity that is bound to occur, especially since MADD had been so actively involved?" To paraphrase, his response was, "One time is enough." He withdrew from the search process. He had needed someone to pose the question to him and talk about the consequences of the earlier arrest if it became public a second time.

I am deeply troubled by the fact that a poor decision made in one's past can continue to hang over good candidates like a sword suspended by a thread, yet the reality is that old errors may continue to plague both aspiring and experienced candidates. It is a fact that a fingerprinted criminal charge will probably remain with you for life. It is something with which you will have to deal. The impact that a criminal charge will have on your career will depend upon the nature of the charge and whether or not it led to a conviction. If you are dealing with a consultant, it is imperative that you alert her to the issue and at least consider the professional opinion offered.

Lawsuits

In addition to requesting information as it pertains to a possible criminal record, some districts will also inquire if you have been or are currently involved in any lawsuits either as a defendant or plaintiff. Routine matters will not be of concern, but lawsuits that involve you and former employers will need to be explored by the employer. Lawsuits concerning any fiduciary wrongdoing on your part as a school administrator will also be of interest. Some districts may be interested in your credit rating to determine if financial issues will haunt you while in the new position. It is best that you give sufficient detail when answering these questions. If the employer wants more detail, he will ask for it.

I once worked with a candidate who was applying for the position of superintendent of schools in another state and was involved in a lawsuit with a former employer. The interview was in the spring, and the job had a summer start date. The case was to be heard in court in September, about the time the schools in the new district would be opening. Unfortunately, the candidate never informed the board or the consultant about the pending court case. One board member heard a rumor and pursued it in some detail. He then informed the other board members at a meeting during which I was present. It was new information to me.

The candidate did not, in the board's judgment, have the qualifications to lead the district and was not moved forward in the search process. Yet if it had happened that he was the best professionally qualified candidate, how would a board have reacted to the fact that the candidate was not forthcoming regarding the lawsuit? Would this or any other candidate have been eliminated because of an act of omission? Is there an obligation to inform a board about a pending legal matter even if not asked on an application? What would have occurred if the candidate had been appointed and the court case turned out to be nasty and publicized? It is for these reasons that you should consider informing the consultant or potential employer of pending legal matters that could impact the public's perception of its school leader.

Being forthcoming with the facts can work to your advantage. For example, I worked with a candidate who had been arrested and later appointed to a responsible position. He informed the new employer about this at the beginning of the search. His arrest was for a foolish, almost childish, act but one with substantial media coverage. Rather than being silent on the matter, he was forthcoming with the new board during the interview stage. He was able to explain the circumstances that led to his arrest because he took the initiative. Had he not done so, the situation would have placed both him and the board on the defensive. The board understood what had happened and hired him in spite of the arrest on this minor charge. It remained a non-issue because of the candidate's openness.

Sexual or Physical Misconduct

If you have been involved in a sexual or physical misconduct matter, whether or not you were arrested and or convicted, it is a serious matter and will be of concern to a consultant and employer. Background checks in your current school district and in your community of residence will eventually reveal this information. If you choose not to bring it to the attention of the consultant or employer, you must be prepared to deal with the matter when it comes to the public's attention. And you can be assured that it eventually will become a public matter. It is not uncommon to have educators arrested and convicted on sexual abuse charges. If we have educators who engage in such activity, they have no business in education. Furthermore, if they are currently employed in education, they will hopefully be discovered and terminated before they do more harm.

Physical abuse in education is less common, but it occurs. Again, this type of conduct has no place in education and those in positions of responsibility need to be ever vigilant by taking great care before hiring those suspected of such conduct and by terminating those who do engage in it. Because both types of activity are criminal offenses, a background check by a school district that involves a fingerprint check with the FBI and with the state police will most likely reveal this information. A responsible school district will also check with the state department of education in your current and former states to determine if your license to teach or to administer has been terminated or if there is any action pending against you.

Alcohol Abuse

Alcohol abuse could form the basis for eliminating you from contention. While an employer may be required to assist you with an alcohol-related problem if you are a current member of the work force, it has no obligation as a potential employer to hire someone with the problem.

Educators have been forced out of jobs because of alcohol abuse on school property. Often, those who abuse alcohol find themselves in automobile accidents or being stopped for erratic driving. When a public figure is arrested for driving while under the influence, it is news and often leads to the person stepping down from a prominent position. We have witnessed many important public figures forced from their positions because of embarrassing events caused by alcohol abuse. If you drink, it is best that you do not drive. If you choose to drive, you need to limit the amount of alcohol you consume.

It should be obvious that you must not consume alcohol during the school day on school property. However, it is also important that you not consume alcohol while on any kind of school business during your normal workday.

As serious as alcohol abuse is in a school setting, it is also a fact that if a candidate has overcome an alcohol problem, the chances are good that it will not interfere with future employment. Alcohol abuse is one of those issues that needs to be discussed with your search consultant.

Extramarital Affairs

During my ten years as a consultant, I worked with two superintendent candidates who were involved in extramarital affairs at the time they applied for superintendent positions. This information was not known either by the consultant or potential employers at the outset of the search. Interestingly enough, each was from a state that was at least 1,000 miles from the districts in which they had applied. Both affairs became known once the names of the superintendents were announced as semifinalists and the news reached their home communities.

If you apply for a position, and if a serious issue related to you becomes known to the media, an immediate background check will be initiated by the media. The media check will often be more thorough than the one conducted by the potential employer. Members of the media are part of a special brotherhood and sisterhood wherein they share information across all local and state boundaries. The same can be said for teacher associations. When you think of it, the National Teacher Association has what amounts to a branch office in practically every city, town, and hamlet in the United States. There is nothing in your professional past that even the smallest teacher association in the country cannot learn about through its network. As a candidate, you are subject to the greatest of scrutiny.

These two extramarital cases were particularly serious because each male superintendent had an affair with the chairwoman of the board for which he worked. The publicity surrounding these two cases led to four careers being seriously damaged: the resignations of the two superintendents and two chairwomen. In both cases, the preliminary background checks did not discover these indiscretions because no one spoke publicly about them in their respective communities. But once the names of the two men were publicized as being finalists in other communities, their affairs were brought to the attention of the hiring communities. Apparently, there were individuals in the home communities of the superintendents and chairpersons who felt the matter should be made public. In both cases, the consultant and the hiring boards were caught off guard.

Nonrenewal and Termination of Services

This guide makes no attempt to focus on the legal issues surrounding either termination or nonrenewal. Termination, in particular, is a complex matter compounded by the diverse approaches taken in each state. Any attempt to summarize state statutes would be futile. Therefore, this guide will only deal with the impact that nonrenewal and termination have on a candidate's future job hunts.

Nonrenewal is a more routine activity than termination, especially as it impacts teachers who, for one reason or other, do not live up to the expectations of the district. I stress to candidates that they must learn to turn down job offers if the chances of success in the district that offered a contract are minimal. Some districts do not possess the financial or human resources to provide the support that new employees require. In other districts nonrenewal may be part of the culture.

Nonrenewal is also a common occurrence in districts that automatically nonrenew all nontenured teachers as a matter of practice pending a final district budget. In other cases, nonrenewal is used to reduce staff.

If an application asks if you have been terminated or nonrenewed, you need to answer the question truthfully. The district will eventually learn of it when a background check is conducted. Once nonrenewal or termination is noted on the application, the employer will require details.

If you have been nonrenewed for reasons other than a routine district practice of nonrenewing all nontenured teachers or as a result of a legitimate reduction in force, you need to give thought as to how you will explain this to a potential employer. You need to do this well in advance of submitting the application. My suggestion (oftentimes taken, many times ignored) is to prepare a detailed narrative to attach to the application. A colleague who has a thorough understanding of your situation should be asked to review the narrative. If a consultant is involved, you should ask his opinion as to how the narrative reads. The employer will understand that it is written from your perspective. However, if the employer is interested in your candidacy, the accuracy of your statement will speak volumes about your professionalism and integrity.

If you were nonrenewed or terminated for ethical, moral, or real or suspected illegal fiduciary reasons, you have a serious problem. In this case, you need to have professional and legal advice regarding your next step. You must face the fact that you may have become unemployable in the education field.

A Vote Not to Extend

Superintendents are often in a situation where, unlike a governing board action to nonrenew, they are subject to an action by the governing board that decides "not to extend" a contract. The distinction between action for nonrenewal and board action not to extend can be important depending upon specific circumstances. Nonrenewal occurs most often when a superintendent is in the last year of a multiple-year contract; the governing board makes it clear that the current year is to be the last year and formalizes it, voting publicly not to renew the person's contract.

An action not to extend a contract usually occurs when a superintendent is operating under a multiple-year contract and each year requests the board to extend it for another year. For example, take the case of a superintendent with a three-year contract. At the end of the first year, the superintendent requests that another year be added to the contract so that it remains three years in length. She usually requests this every year. Sooner or later, the governing board may either vote formally not to extend, or it may remain silent on the superintendent's request, which has the same effect as not extending the contract. However, a board's remaining silent is of benefit to the employee in most cases because the matter is kept out of the public arena. When this occurs, the superintendent has to determine why the board took the action it did. If it was over an issue or matter that can be resolved, the superintendent may stay on for another year and attempt to earn an extension. If he determines that the board would like for him to leave, then the superintendent usually begins a job hunt. It is not unusual for a board to decline to be specific as to why it did not want to extend a contract, in which case the superintendent is faced with a dilemma: to stay or begin a search.

A recent incident underscores the importance of being truthful when you are involved in a board action not to extend. A superintendent was hired under a three-year contract. During the second and third years of the contract, he asked that it be extended so that it always was three years in length. His board honored the requests. During the fourth year of his employment, the board voted not to extend the contract, thus leaving the superintendent with two full years plus the few months left in the current year. There were no ethical, moral, or financial issues involved. Quite the opposite; the candidate was totally professional. Because the superintendent was not particularly happy in the district, several months before the vote was taken not to extend his contract, he met with a consultant at a national convention to explore other opportunities. At the time of the meeting with the consultant, no action had been taken by the superintendent's board not to extend. Thus, there was nothing to share with the consultant on that matter.

Two or three months after the board voted not to extend the superintendent's contract, the consultant, unaware of the vote, contacted the superintendent to inform him that he was invited to be interviewed for a superintendent position in a different region of the country. The superintendent accepted the invitation to be interviewed. He was one of four candidates. The conditions were such that all four interviews would be held on a Monday or Tuesday. The four candidates were then expected to remain in the area where they could be contacted late on Tuesday afternoon. If any were determined to be finalists, they would return for a Wednesday interview.

The superintendent asked for my advice since we had known each other professionally for several years. The call was made to me a few days before his interview. He related the facts as stated above and which I subsequently learned were accurate. The question was, when should he have informed the consultant and the interviewing board of his recent nonrenewal? I thought about it at length, and we discussed several scenarios. But in the end, I suggested that he complete the first interview and say nothing at that time. If he was invited back for the Wednesday interview, he could then call the consultant and ask to meet with him either late Tuesday or early Wednesday before the interview and then lay out the new facts. The candidate did just that. The lesson learned in this case is that a candidate must be forthright with the consultant and the board, as was done in this case. The candidate made all of the right moves. Unsure of what to do, he sought advice and followed it.

In the case of administrators, especially superintendents, being nonrenewed or terminated is not a professional tragedy if either occurred for the right reason. It happens to many. Becoming reemployed will be more difficult but not impossible. The development of a narrative that describes what happened is crucial to a new job search. It must be accurate and the reader has to be convinced that you were on the correct moral and ethical side of the issue that led to nonrenewal or termination. Many times, the nonrenewal or termination may have nothing to do with you but rather with a board agenda that was not made known to you upon hiring.

A nonrenewal or termination of a superintendent is often due to poor interpersonal skills that manifest themselves in a top-down management style. I mentioned earlier that highly honed interpersonal skills are a distinct intelligence that not all leaders possess. Education, at least at the administrative level, is a service industry where strong relationships are vital to effective team building. Interestingly enough, if an extensive background check is made, a person's history of not possessing outstanding interpersonal skills is almost always discovered. Breakdown in the background process oftentimes occur when board members conduct a site visit without the expertise of the consultant or fail to develop a site visit agenda that is designed to dig deeply into a candidate's background.

I personally know of numerous cases where superintendents have been nonrenewed. In many instances, I have worked with these same superintendents as they sought new employment. Many (if not most) of them had earned the right to serve again. A few did not earn renewal. A handful should never have been in the educational field at all.

There are four lessons to be learned about nonrenewal, termination, and an action not to extend:

First, the reason for the action taken by the district will be important to any district to which you apply. You need to develop an accurate narrative about the matter.

Second, if the action taken was for moral, ethical, or fiduciary failings that were proven, you will have a difficult time becoming reemployed.

Third, if nonrenewal was for a routine reduction in force, you will not be tainted by the nonrenewal action.

Fourth, it always pays to seek good counsel, usually professional and occasionally legal, before you proceed in your job hunt if you were non-renewed, terminated, or subject to a vote not to extend your contract.

If you are not renewed or if terminated, it will serve you well if you write an explanatory narrative. The narrative, if forthright, will help immensely in clarifying your thoughts and help set a new personal course. The length of the document depends upon the issues and complexities involved. It is not intended that the narrative will justify wrongdoing or improprieties; rather, it is for those who rightly believe they deserve a second chance. Such a narrative will also be of assistance to anyone to whom you may turn for professional and legal help.

5

A STAR IS BORN

It is both intriguing and discouraging to witness how poorly most candidates present themselves on paper. Resumes and cover letters tend to be unacceptable, often needing major reengineering. Minor editing usually is not adequate. The most experienced candidates, many of whom have not been in the job market for years, tend to produce some of the poorest documents. Given the poor quality of their documents, it is small wonder that any of them make it through the initial stage of a job search. Given what some candidates present, it is easy and justifiable for a consultant and employer to eliminate them at the outset.

What most candidates fail to realize is that a resume is a biography, a story that affords the opportunity to tell others about you. It is the forum to display talent, experience, and training. It is intended to highlight important elements of your career, a way to move ahead of those who do not take the time to prepare an effective and interesting biography. Because it is a story, you need to tell it in an interesting and logical way. You are encouraged to use the services of a professional in your field to assess the effectiveness of your resume.

Aspiring administrators, usually teachers without any administrative experience or those in entry-level administrative positions, are often at a loss to identify sufficient information to include in a resume or cover letter. One way to address this shortcoming is to engage in extra tasks in your present position. The best advice you can receive at this early stage in your administrative quest is that if you are not participating in activities in your school beyond your classroom activities, then you need to begin now. You need to stand out from the crowd. You need to distinguish yourself in ways that other aspiring administrators do not. A star must be born! It needs to be the brightest of all stars in this job-hunt galaxy. You are the only person with the capability of giving birth to this new star.

I also find that many teachers and administrators in entry-level positions often do not give themselves sufficient credit for their fine works. When I engage them in a personal conversation, I often discover that they have interesting elements in their background and that they underestimate the value of these elements to potential employers.

THREE ESSENTIAL QUESTIONS

Before you begin to create your resume, take time to answer the following questions:

1. Who is your audience?
2. What are the members of the audience looking for in the candidate?
3. What is it that you must emphasize in a resume to attract the attention of the audience?

CREATING A RESUME

It is important to construct your resume in such a way that you can easily create several versions in order to emphasize different strengths to different employers. Given the ease of creating documents quickly and efficiently on a computer, this is not difficult.

My Golden Rule of Resume Writing

The Herbert William Consulting golden rule of resume writing is that if you haven't accomplished it, attended it, earned it, worked there, been there, read it, created it, or been a colleague, then don't mention it! The media and adversaries love to find discrepancies.

Your initial goal in creating the resume is to begin by telling the truth. Telling the truth also implies not exaggerating to the point where you are flirting with fabrication. You are expected to put your best foot forward. However, anything you state on a resume is subject to a background check and to the scrutiny of an interviewer. If you falsify your resume and are appointed to the position, the resume is then subject to the scrutiny of the media. If you are caught in a lie, you may experience the end of your career both as a candidate and as an employee. Just as alcohol abuse has destroyed the careers of public officials, the same is true with those who fabricate credentials and place them in a resume or application.

When you have completed a draft of your resume, have it edited and scrutinized by someone who has had experience with the hiring process. If you work with a consultant, he may be helpful. Whomever you select, it is vital that you have it read by someone who is impartial and who can provide valuable feedback. A good resume is like good grooming: it will not necessarily get you the job but it will keep you in the running. A poor resume is like poor grooming: it could lose you an opportunity to compete.

There are many commercial packages available to assist you in writing a resume. Use them as guidelines and then prepare a personalized resume to fit your qualifications that catches the attention of the reader. Except in specific areas of labor shortage, the chances are that your resume will be examined for only a few minutes before an initial judgment is made as to whether it will enter the "in," "out," or "maybe" basket. Therefore, create the resume with those classifications in mind.

I stress, during private job-coaching sessions, that the resume be kept simple and clean. Let the words and your accomplishments speak for themselves. I find that different size font, the overuse of **highlighting**, *italics*, bullets, and <u>underlining</u> serve only to distract the reader.

Resume Categories

There are no standards as to what should be included in a resume. However, there are several categories that you need to consider. They include:

1. Heading
2. Professional experience

3. Full-time employment
   Part-time employment
   Multiple titles
   Title inflation
4. Educational Background
5. Certifications and Licenses
6. Professional Affiliations
7. Selected Accomplishments
8. Professional Contributions and Writings
9. Awards Received
10. Civic Contributions
11. Interests
12. Addendum
13. References

Heading

At the top of the first page you need to place your full name, including middle initial, maiden name, aliases, full address including zip, phone and fax numbers including area code, and e-mail address.

Since your job hunt is for a specific position, you do not need to write a short description of the position you are seeking or your career objective on the resume. The position you applied for is your present career objective. Do not talk about the next step in your career unless asked about it. If you are asked, be modest and talk only about the very next step and not your final career goals.

Professional Experience

A question frequently raised by a candidate is "what is an effective format for a resume and what goes in what order?" As a consultant, I have examined resumes prepared in a variety of formats, with the sequence of events ordered in many ways. In my opinion, list the most important information on the resume first. In education, that information is professional experience. My sense is that the same is true of all professions. The resume logically should begin with your professional qualifications, listing your current experience first and working backward from there.

As you list current and past employers, be certain to provide accurate names and addresses of the districts or schools you worked in and the complete titles of supervisors. Consultants and potential employers do not have the time to seek out information you should have included. They are not paid to do your work.

Full-Time Experience You must be particularly careful how you record dates of employment. If you use only full years without months you have the opportunity to literally "hide" an entire year or more. For example, consider the following employment dates for this candidate.

Worked in District A, 1991–1992
Worked in District B, 1992–1995
Worked in District C, 1995–2002

At first glance, it appears that the candidate had been employed continuously from 1991 through 1992 in District A—but she could have worked from December 1991 to January 1992, a period of only two months!

Similarly, this candidate could have worked from December 1992 to January 1995 in District B, a total of twenty-six months instead of the forty-eight months implied in using the dates 1992 to 1995.

While on a six-month consulting assignment to hire several administrators for the same district, I came across an application that was submitted for an assistant superintendent position. The application caught my eye because of the manner in which the applicant recorded his experiences. It was similar to the format illustrated above. He recorded the years and not the months. I remembered him as having had a very short career as a superintendent in another state. I did not know him personally but I knew the name and the circumstances of his employment. He had been let go before the end of his first year as superintendent. On his new application he did as described above in an attempt to hide a ten-month assignment that had ended badly. I scheduled an interview with him and asked him if he had ever worked as a superintendent. He answered "no." For all practical purposes, his interview was over.

A more positive example occurred while, as superintendent, I was recruiting someone for an elementary classroom position. The finalist was well qualified and recommended by the building principal. A previously conducted background check validated our positive impression of her credentials. By the time I interviewed her, the staff had determined that she should be offered a contract unless some serious issue were to arise during her final interview. In the course of that interview, I asked about the dates of employment listed on her application. She, too, had used only years without months, and it became obvious that the better part of a year was missing. When asked about it, she was clearly embarrassed. It happened that she was single and had spent the better part of a year traveling with her boyfriend in Europe and was afraid that if she let this be known she would not have been hired. She would have been better off to list the year as professional travel. Nevertheless, she was offered a contract that she accepted.

The lesson to be learned about dates is to be accurate when recording them on a resume and application. It takes little time to enter the months as well as the years. By doing so, the consultant and employer have a reasonable assurance that all employment has been listed accurately, with all time accounted for.

Part-Time Positions   It is common practice in education for candidates to have held a number of part-time positions while pursuing a full-time career. For example, many administrators pursue adjunct professor positions at local universities while holding down a full-time position in a school district. You need to list part-time positions so that they make sense chronologically to the reader. You can do this in two ways. At the end of a resume you can include a section "Other Employment" in which you list part-time positions or unusual jobs you have had in addition to your regular position, or you can list them in chronological order in the professional experience section.

Remember that the resume is prepared for the reader not the writer. What makes sense to you may be confusing to the reader. Therefore, always create a resume from the viewpoint of the reader.

Multiple Titles   It is not uncommon for some employees to hold two or more titles. For example, you may be a principal of a middle school and also be fulfilling a central office function, such as coordinator of instruction. You must display both positions in an order that makes chronological sense since you may have held the positions for different periods of time. For example, you may have been principal from July 1, 1995, to June 30, 2003, but your time as coordinator was from August 1, 1997 to March 1, 2001. Do you insert the second title and assignment before or after the full-time position? While there is no correct answer, it is logical to place the primary experience first, in this case the principal position, and then list the coordinator assignment following it.

Title Inflation   One area where candidates often stretch the truth is when recording job titles. It may happen when a candidate does not believe he has impressive enough credentials and feels the need to exaggerate. The rule of thumb is that the title you use on a resume or application should be the same title used on the district's organization chart or as recorded on your employment contract. Positions held that are in addition to a regular job, such as co-chair of a curriculum committee or team leader, should be titled on the resume and application with the same accuracy as you record your full-time position.

Educational Background

Educational background logically follows experience on the resume. The reason I suggest this order is that the reader will find it convenient to compare, chronologically, your experience and your education. This is especially convenient when both categories appear on the first page of the resume. It answers questions about what impact degrees earned had on your career. It also answers questions as to why you might have gaps in your work history. However, there is no harm done if you list education first. Mostly, it is a matter of preference.

I have been involved in several cases where applicants have fraudulently listed degrees earned. Most employers will at some stage in the process request copies of your transcripts and diplomas. If you have not earned a degree, do not list it. In the cases that have come to my attention, the abuses related solely to the fraudulent listing of graduate degrees.

The one area where I find professional abuse, as opposed to fraudulent abuse, is with the recording of doctoral work. Unlike a fraudulent listing, candidates tend to overstate the status of their doctoral work. Far more educators are enrolled in doctoral programs than will ever earn a degree. The dropout rate is high, primarily because many doctoral candidates never complete the dissertation. A high percentage complete most course work and then quit. When it comes to the application and resume, some candidates who have engaged in doctoral work but who have not earned the degree will use creative wording to mislead the reader. The candidates want to leave the impression that the degree has been earned, that the level of work completed is greater that the facts will bear out, or that they are still enrolled in a program when in fact they are out of the program. You are urged to be accurate in describing your doctoral program status. And never use ABD (all but dissertation), which few readers ever understand.

Certifications and Licenses

Being properly certified or licensed to teach or administer is a major requirement in every state. Therefore, it is essential that you list on the application *and* resume all the certifications you possess plus any other licenses and endorsements that are pertinent to this job hunt. The consultant and employer are obviously most interested in certifications and licenses you hold in the state in which you are applying. Certificates issued in other states are important if there is reciprocity between the two states. They also provide the potential employer with information about the areas you might qualify for if they are interested in you and if there is time for you to apply for certification in the new state.

Professional Affiliations

As an inexperienced candidate, you may not have many professional affiliations to list. However, if you plan on advancing your career, you must become active in professional associations, especially those in your subject or professional interest areas. All too often, an inexperienced candidate will defer becoming involved in professional associations because of the cost of membership. However, this is a case of where you pay now or pay later with a resume that lacks depth. Experienced candidates usually have a number of affiliations to list. While these affiliations do not guarantee you a position, they provide an indication of your level of activity and interest in the profession. There is little excuse for any candidate not to be active in at least one professional association.

Selected Accomplishments

Candidates who have thought ahead about a career move will make it a point to engage in other activities that bring professional attention to their work. I refer to this category of the resume as "selected accomplishments." What are such accomplishments? They can include:

- Collaboration with local museums or nonprofit foundations
- Writing grants for the district
- Taking leadership positions with civic organizations
- Designing professional development programs
- Mentoring younger teachers and administrators
- Working with the elderly in your community

There is no end to the type of selected professional and voluntary accomplishment opportunities available to you. They exist in every community and school district and are as varied as one's imagination. There are innumerable organizations that are constantly seeking volunteer help. What it takes is initiative on your part, always keeping in mind that you want to be able to distinguish yourself. You want to expand the professional distance between you and the other candidates for the position you seek. This can be a vital section of your resume.

Professional Contributions and Writings

A section on professional contributions/writings provides an opportunity to note any work you have undertaken with other organizations as a presenter, and to list articles or professional writings you have had published. Employers are always interested in the degree to which you understand your subject area and have shared that knowledge with others. This section requires that you be accurate in listing your publications, providing sufficient information for the consultant and employer to research and validate your work. As is the case with selected accomplishments, professional contributions and writings require you to take the initiative to seek out opportunities where you are able to excel. Documents and newsletters created for internal organizational use are not considered professional writings, but list them anyway and be prepared to offer copies if requested to do so.

Awards Received

Awards received are one indication that peers and supervisors respect you and have given public acknowledgment to your success. Every profession, especially education, provides many opportunities to participate in activities that can lead to an award being bestowed upon you. Although this section may be a short one, depending upon your experience, it is still another way to bring attention to your accomplishments. Opportunities to compete for awards are available at the district and state levels, and through the many private foundations that support teaching and administrative efforts. Once again, you need to demonstrate your initiative.

Civic Contributions

It is common practice for educators to take an interest in community organizations. Many see such activities as an extension of their vocation. Membership itself is not the important factor; rather, it is the degree to which you participated in the functions of the organization. Being a member of Rotary is one thing, being the president of the organization or the chair of a major fund-raising committee is quite another thing. When a decision is to be made as to which of two outstanding candidates will be offered a position, activities such as these might make the difference. Your contributions to these organizations often signal to the employer that you are willing to take on tasks that others avoid.

Interests

A resume would not be complete without a category to list your interests. When you are pursuing your first administrative position, you usually do not have much of a history to display on a resume. Therefore, the "interests" category may catch the eye of readers. A caution is necessary: If you do not actively participate in a specific activity, do *not* list it. For example, if you say that you engage in mountain climbing, as distinct from hiking up mountains, be certain you actually do "climb" because someone on the interviewing committee may be a skilled climber and engage you in a discussion on the technical aspects of the sport.

Most candidates will list activities such as "travel, tennis, reading" and similar hobbies as other interests. While interesting, they are hardly eye-catching or memorable. A careful analysis of what you do in your free time may bring forth an overlooked but exciting activity. I'm reminded of a client with limited professional experience who told me that he had nothing of real interest to list. During the interview, I learned that on weekends he was engaged in his private photography endeavors, something he failed to mention on his resume. I further learned that not only was he interested in photography but he also provided aerial photography services for private companies with need for such information. I believed an employer would be interested in a candidate who had such an interesting avocation. Importantly, when he discussed aerial photography, he became more animated than when he talked about his educational career. I emphasized to him that he needed to bring that same enthusiasm to other aspects of his job hunt.

Addendum

An "Addendum" is used in special cases. It is a category that affords the candidate an opportunity to add more detail without detracting from the basic resume. Over the years, I have kept note on how resumes differ among administrative candidates. All tend to make similar mistakes but with one major difference. Some make their resumes much more extensive, for example, by listing every conference, lecture, in-service workshop, seminar, and workshop they attended, and by further detailing the more minute aspects of their work. It is not unusual for this listing to take up to two to three pages. It is a well-meaning effort and is done in order to demonstrate to the consultant and employer that they are well qualified for a position. Unfortunately, this format tends to make resumes less attractive because of length. It is distracting to have to wade your way through all of the mundane information to get to the heart of the resume. While the resume is meant to be a story, it is not meant to be an itemized educational history. What I recommend is an addendum to the resume in which these details can be listed without distracting from the recommended two-page main resume.

References

It is not necessary to list the names of references on a resume unless requested to do so. In education, the application form used by a school district will generally ask for references. The resume can address the references from two different angles. One is to simply note that "References are available upon request" and the other is to have a separate attachment to the resume with references if you wish to include them. The reason for the separate attachment is that it can be altered without changing the resume. If you do list references, either in the resume or as an attachment, be certain the list is up-to-date and that those listed have been made aware that they are being listed. Phone numbers need to be accurate, including area codes, and both home and office numbers should be listed, if available. You must make it convenient for the consultant or employer to reach your references. The guideline relative to references is that any person listed must have a good understanding of your work, be a professional reference rather than a personal one, be aware of the position for which you have applied, and be prepared to speak positively of your work.

References can be very important in a job search. A colleague of mine recently interviewed for an administrative position at an area college. The chair of the hiring committee told him following the interview, that he (the chair) had contacted one of the references the candidate listed. The reference happened to be president of another area college. The chair of the interviewing committee then said, "The president's recommendation was all you needed to clinch this job!" That was the only reference called. So it is still true, for good or ill, that who you know does matter.

COVER LETTER

Four out of five cover letters submitted are poorly written and do more to eliminate rather than promote a candidate. Most letters are far too lengthy. Most candidates do not write well and, consequently, the cover letter only serves to expose their linguistic deficiencies. For that reason, I suggest several guidelines for writing cover letters.

Heading

The information at the top of your cover letter should be the same as on your resume. Do not confuse the reader with different information or a different format or style. Proof both headings to make certain they are identical. For some reason, applicants tend to provide less information in the cover letter heading than they do in the resume heading. You need to think in terms of documents being separated from one another in the review process. Each should stand alone in terms of the information needed to contact you.

The First Sentence and Length of Letter

The first sentence in a cover letter should come close to saying it all. "I am applying for the position of assistant principal of the Brown School. Please accept this letter and attachments as my formal application." Rarely do I see a cover letter with an opening sentence that is direct in its message.

Then keep the letter short. The more you write, the more apt you are to make mistakes. In my opinion, a cover letter longer than one page is too long. An exception to the length may occur when the application consists only of a cover letter and resume. If this is the case, the cover letter will need to be more extensive since it takes the place of a formal application.

Technically, it is suggested that you use one-inch margins, 12-point font, no highlighting, and no bullets, italics, or underlining anywhere on the page, including your letterhead. Under no circumstances are you to use school district letterhead or envelopes. This is a personal job search, and you are to keep it that way.

The cover letter is the first document I examine when I receive an application from a candidate or when I am coaching clients. I want it short, articulate, and focused. I want to learn in the letter what a candidate did not or could not express in the resume. From your perspective, it is vital that the letter sets you apart from all the other candidates by noting one or two attributes that you possess that other candidates in similar positions typically will not possess. I want to know that I not only have a well-educated candidate but also a learned one.

You should make the assumption that if you advance to the next step in the process, others involved in the recruiting effort will read your letter. Each will have an opinion about it; some will focus on what you said, others on how you stated it, while a few will be correcting the letter for grammar, spelling, and punctuation.

Sample Rewrite

The following are the two sentences used in a recent cover letter a candidate submitted to me during a private job-coaching session. I think you will agree that if the original sentences had remained in his cover letter during his quest for a position, it would not have been well received.

The first sentence read: "This letter of application is in reference to the high school principal opening in the Brown Public Schools."

The rewrite read:

"Please accept this letter and attachments as my formal application for the position of high school principal at the Brown School. I will forward other documents as requested."

The rewrite is more definitive in that the candidate states clearly why he is writing, namely, to be a formal candidate. Rather than being a letter written in "reference" to the opening, he is stating in his new letter that he is a candidate.

The second sentence the candidate first submitted to me read:

Working currently as a high school principal and with other diversified experience as a middle school principal; assistant middle school principal; elementary principal; Ohio Service Center Training Laboratory and Utah ACES Technology Division as a staff development trainer; mathematics and biology learning facilitator; reading workshop leader; Wisconsin teacher assessor, mentor and cooperating teacher and classroom teacher of ten years, I feel confident that I'm capable of fulfilling this position.

Because there were several thoughts stated in the above sentence, it was suggested that it be divided into two separate ideas.

The first part of the divided sentence then read:

> I believe I am particularly qualified for this position having served both as a middle school principal and middle school assistant principal in (Blank). In addition, I have had the experience of working in a 10–12 high school and a K–4 elementary school. With this broad range of experiences across many grades, I understand the unique place that each grade and subject has in the experience of each child.

What is important in this new sentence is that he highlighted the fact that he has had experience in all grades except grade 5 and 9. This range of experiences is unique, and it is a background that the employer will find interesting. Few candidates will possess this range of experience.

Then, the new second sentence read:

> My experiences in the (Former) Public School System and at the Utah ACES Technology Division in the field of technology provided me with a strong background in a discipline that constantly needs strengthening in most school systems. I am skilled at training teachers and administrators in a variety of technology areas.

The second sentence is interesting to the employer because the candidate has now distanced himself from most other candidates with his ability to train teachers and administrators in technology areas. This is an added skill he would bring to an administrative position.

The Last Sentence in the Letter

The closing of a letter is as important as the beginning. It needs to be direct. It is the last thought you leave with the employer or consultant. As you prepare to bring closure to this communication, ask yourself, "What is it that I want from this cover letter?" What you want, of course, is an interview! Close the letter with that thought: "I look forward to the opportunity to meet with you to further discuss my candidacy."

This chapter was written to remind candidates of one simple fact when preparing a resume: it is a story to be told in a manner that the reader will find both interesting and intriguing. Each of us is a star in our own right. The resume is an opportunity to illuminate it, making it shine brighter than all the other stars with whom we compete. A candidate cannot help but be successful if he has worked to create quality experiences and reports them in an honest, forthright, interesting, and professional manner.

As was stated earlier, the golden rule of resume writing is that "if you haven't accomplished it, attended it, earned it, worked there, been there, read it, created it, or been a colleague of, then don't mention it!" The media and adversaries love to find discrepancies in the application materials of candidates applying for important public jobs.

Think of the cover letter as a written introduction to the consultant or employer, and the resume as a written interview. Now that you have acquired guidelines for the preparation of a resume and cover letter, let us move on to the preparation of the application form, seeking appropriate letters of reference, and following up on materials mailed.

6

PERFECT APPLICATIONS REQUIRED

Having processed thousands of applications, both for my firm and for employers, I safely estimate that approximately 50 percent of those who apply for positions do not completely follow the instructions on the application. As consultants, we want what we want when we want it. It is that simple. The same holds true for an employer who has to make comparisons between many applicants and therefore needs data submitted in the same format. Following instructions is essential. It only takes a few more minutes to complete the application with perfection. You simply do what the employer has requested. If you are unresponsive at this stage of the search, an employer or consultant worries that you will be unresponsive once hired. You should not set yourself up to be eliminated at the outset of a job hunt because of your failure to submit an application that is accurate and complete.

BIOGRAPHICAL DATA

It is vital that an applicant provide accurate biographical data. The consultant or employer needs a full name, address including zip code, home and business phone numbers including area code, Social Security number, maiden name, and other alias that you may have used. It is also appropriate to add other data such as cell phone, fax, and e-mail address. If you do not want to be contacted at work, you must indicate this on the application.

For reasons of privacy, some candidates may be reluctant to list a Social Security number, but many employers use it as a way to record and track applications. It is often the only way for an employer to access and validate certification status with your state certification office. Without proper certification, many consultants and employers will not move your candidacy forward.

Contractual Information

In the case of administrators who work under individual contracts, particularly superintendents and others at the top of the organizational chart, questions may be raised relating to length of contract, when last renewed, current expiration date, and salary. The point is to determine if the candidate is currently employed or if there was a refusal on the part of the employer to renew the current contract when it expired. If you are in a search where these questions are asked, you need to answer them accurately and truthfully.

In chapter 4, it was mentioned that if you are being nonrenewed or have been terminated, you should prepare a narrative that describes the reasons why a district took the action it did and describing other circumstances that are important for an employer to know in judging your application. The narrative is also helpful to you in clarifying your thoughts about the issue. Depending upon the circumstances, the document may or may not be shared with the consultant or employer, although the contents will need to be discussed.

Certification Information

You will be asked to list your certification(s) in the state in which you are applying. You must do so. If you do not have proper certification, do not ignore the request for information but simply state you do not possess the certification required. This is important because many states do not have reciprocity. Without appropriate certification, you may not be employable. To be considered a serious candidate, you must have demonstrated some effort to acquire certification. You must be forward thinking and plan a strategy to become certified. We eliminate many candidates because they do not possess proper certification or have not made any effort to acquire it.

If you are interested in working in a particular state(s), you should initiate efforts to acquire certification long before you apply for a position. Attach to the application all correspondence you have had with the appropriate state certification office so that the reviewer can determine if you are serious about competing for the position for which you have applied. It is a way to validate a candidate's integrity. All too often a candidate from out of state will indicate he has applied for certification when in fact that is not the case. Employers do not want to learn that you "are going to apply for certification"; rather, they want to know that you have already applied. At the time you apply for a position, it is expected that, at a minimum, you would have requested a certification application and then submitted it to the state certification office for processing. If you already possess the required certification, attach copies to the application.

Experience

Every application will ask for your experience record and a listing of all positions, including your current one. Rarely will you have room to list all positions, but the most current experiences are the most important. Your resume will provide your complete employment record. Under no circumstances are you to simply write in this section of the application "See resume." If a consultant or employer wants to use the resume to review your work experience, they would have stated that. Of all the instructions given on an application, this is the one most frequently ignored. If the instructions state you are to list positions starting with the most recent, that is exactly what they mean.

WRITING SAMPLE

Although not as popular as it used to be, an essay is occasionally requested as part of the application process. If not requested as part of the application, it is sometimes required of the finalists. Many candidates tend to ignore the writing of an original essay when requested and simply attach a piece of writing created for another publication or for internal use in his district. This is an early warning sign to the consultant or employer that the candidate is not serious about seeking this particular position. Providing what is not wanted is worse than not providing what is requested. Other sections of an application will indicate that specific data be provided on the form. Do not write "see attachment" unless there is no room to provide the requested data on the form.

UNAVAILABLE INFORMATION

If for any reason you are unable to provide what was asked for, you should write a short note explaining why you cannot comply and attach it to the application. It is also appropriate to write the note directly on the application, if there is room. For example, there may be a request to have a letter of recommendation from your immediate supervisor, who may be out of the country for several weeks and unable to provide such a letter. If that happens, and if the search is on a fast track, the employer may ask you to provide another recommendation from a party to be determined by the employer.

LETTERS OF REFERENCE

Every application will request that letters of references be attached. The request for letters of references often creates a dilemma both for the applicant and the employer. In the case of our firm, we ask for three current letters from professionals who know of your work. They are to be attached to the application.

In addition, we have a section that asks the applicant to list the names, addresses, and phone numbers of three additional professional references. Please note that "letters of reference" are distinct from "names of references." The "names of references" must be different from the names of those who provided the "letters of reference."

We also note on the application that if for any reason a candidate is unable to comply fully with the reference request, all that is required is a phone call to inform us about why the request cannot be met. For example, a superintendent applying for a new position is usually reluctant to ask a current employer for a reference at the beginning of a search because it could compromise the candidate in her own district. Thus, it is understandable that there may not be full compliance with the letter of reference section.

All letters of reference should be dated. The most valuable are usually those that are current. Do not overwhelm the district or consultant with more letters of reference than are requested. An early warning sign to a consultant that things may not be going well for a candidate is when we are overwhelmed with letters of reference, especially if they are old or undated letters. If and when additional references are required, they will be requested.

You must exert caution when you attach letters of reference. Not all letters you perceive as positive are interpreted that way by the consultant or employer, who are usually skilled at reading between the lines. Before you attach letters, have an objective third party read them and determine if they will support your candidacy. If not, acquire other letters. Simply because a letter of reference is from a noted educator, professor, or administrator does not automatically mean it is well written or that it makes a positive statement about your work.

Allow me to share a story with you of a candidate for a central office position and his letters of reference. He submitted three letters of reference to my office. As members of my staff were reading them, one employee noted that, although different administrators in the candidate's district allegedly wrote them, there was a similar tone to all of them. My employee then examined the letters more closely, and it was apparent that all three were written on the same machine. Further compounding this issue was the fact that the candidate had used school system letterhead for all three letters. One of the three letters was from the candidate's superintendent. I called the superintendent and asked if he had written the letter. He knew nothing about it. It was then learned that the candidate had written all three letters himself. In spite of his efforts, he could not disguise his writing style sufficiently to pull off this fraud.

Additional Reference Information

As mentioned above, you will most likely be requested to list the names and phone numbers of additional references whom the consultant or employer can contact. If you do not want the consultant or employer to contact references at this stage in the process, it is proper protocol for you to attach a note in this section. Some candidates often make this request in their cover letter. I suggest that the cover letter only be used as a backup on this matter. If the cover letter becomes separated from an application, it may not be known that you do not want contact made with a specific reference. For that reason, I suggest that the note be placed on the application itself. If you are concerned that your name will inadvertently become known to the public, do not list references; rather, place a statement in the space provided explaining your problem.

Appropriate References

Whom should you use as references? The simple answer is only those persons who can promote your interests as a candidate. Those writing letters need to be clear about your qualifications for the position you applied for. Therefore, the most important references are your immediate supervisors or, in the case of a school superintendent, the chairperson of the board; then, previous supervisors followed by other professionals who are familiar with your work and with whom you have worked. The least important references are professionals who are evaluated by you, the clergy, politicians, and parents. Using peers as a reference is appropriate only if they have worked closely with you on specific projects. The fact that they are in the same department or in the same grade level does not carry much weight with those evaluating your credentials. The use of parents as references for teachers is appropriate since parents constitute their primary constituency.

When contacting references to request letters, you should provide them with an idea of the areas of your professional background that you would like emphasized. A little prompting may go a long way.

Never use unpredictable references simply because of their standing or professional reputation. Do not list someone as a reference if there is any possibility that she may be applying for the same position for which you are applying. For example, I have had both a building principal and superintendent from the same district apply for a superintendent opening in another community. Two problems resulted, one for them and one for me. First, the principal requested a letter of reference from his superintendent with whom he was competing. He received a solid recommendation. The superintendent, however, was not in a position to ask his principal for a reference. Second, I was managing a situation in which both boss and subordinate were applying for the same position, with the superintendent knowing about the principal's candidacy but with the principal in the dark about his superintendent's intentions.

REVIEW OF APPLICATION AND FOLLOW-UP CALL

When you believe that the application is ready to be submitted, it is time to have it reviewed by someone who will provide worthwhile feedback to you. At this stage of the search, you are so involved in completing the application that you are apt to miss errors. Most of us have had the experience of submitting an application only to find errors after it was out of our hands. Do not be reluctant to engage a third party to review the material.

Once you have mailed the application, follow up with a phone call a week to ten days later to be certain that it was received. Do not wait until the last minute to mail your application since it could be held up in the mail and not received in time. Not complying with due dates could result in your not being considered. Hand-delivered materials are more likely to be misplaced than those that are mailed since the recruiting system, especially in a large district with a human relations department, is usually set up to process materials that are mailed.

It pays to take time a week or so after mailing the application to place a call to the district to determine if it arrived. Making personal contact with the human relations department, particularly the secretary in charge of applications, is a good investment of your time. Being polite and courteous to this person will invariably become known to his supervisor, who may be making the decision as to whether or not your application progresses past stage one. A discourteous or aggressive attitude towards a secretary could well push you out of the running. Secretaries are very sensitive to callers who are disrespectful, and have no compunction about talking to others in the office about them. Do not be the one they are complaining about. Leave that onerous reputation to your competitors.

Almost all applications will require an original signature and date. Make certain you comply with this request. Even an honest oversight of this requirement may be cause for concern with the consultant and employer.

PUBLIC SCRUTINY OF APPLICATION MATERIALS

I mentioned earlier that if for any reason your candidacy becomes a high profile one, you can expect that your application, cover letter, and resume will continue to come under scrutiny by employees in the district, the media, and members of the staff and general public. Before you submit an application and related materials, you must be certain that all information is accurate, verifiable, and defensible. This is especially important in the case of those applying for administrative positions. As highly thought of as you may believe you are, there might be individuals who would like nothing better than to catch you fabricating facts. Keep in mind that you are applying for a public position where all application documents will eventually enter the public domain.

7

PLEASE, NO NOTES FROM MOTHER

This guide would not be complete if it failed to address the issue of a candidate turning down a job. Although 99 percent of those reading this guide will be searching for a new job, there are many situations where candidates are offered positions and turn them down or they turn down the opportunity to continue in a job hunt where they are considered by the consultant or employer as the front-runners.

You may rightfully ask, "Does this really happen? After all of the time and energy put into a search, do candidates actually back out at the last minute?" The answer is yes and in doing so, most candidates will employ one of several excuses. I have had candidates refuse a job offer at the eleventh hour, and there are many stories in the search business where candidates have simply walked away from contracts offered.

There are times where turning down a job offer is appropriate, even after an extensive job hunt. For example, a candidate may discover damaging information about a board or district, something that had been hidden from view during the job hunt. A serious unforeseen illness in the family may cause a candidate to step aside in a search. A last-minute glitch in the benefit package or a contract issue that cannot be resolved may be a reason to derail a job hunt. This chapter, however, is dedicated to those occasions when it is *not* appropriate to turn down a job offer. In so doing, a candidate will usually employ one of seven common excuses, none of which are appropriate in turning down a job offer.

All seven of the excuses are less imaginative than the ones we convinced our mothers to write when we cut classes in high school. "Please, no notes from Mother" is a way of stating that, as a consultant or employer, I don't want a candidate using any of the following seven excuses for turning down a job offer at the eleventh hour.

SEVEN COMMON EXCUSES FOR TURNING DOWN JOB OFFERS

These excuses are perfect examples of not letting your head do the walking ahead of time. The reasons listed below as excuses for not accepting a position could have been determined and announced long before you crossed the finish line in first place, or when you found yourself as the chosen front-runner both by the employer and consultant. If any of the seven excuses had been employed at the outset of a search, they would be considered legitimate reasons to turn down a job opportunity. I can't think of a consultant or employer who would not be accepting of them during the early stages of a job hunt. But they are not acceptable when utilized at the end of the process. As you review these seven common excuses, you need to make a commitment that you will not put yourself in a situation where you're looking for your mother to script such an excuse for you.

If you use these excuses, you run the risk of losing the support of your consultant. Early in my career, I used one of them in turning down a superintendent position out of state; in so doing, I lost the support of the country's leading consultant at that time. He was then dean of a prestigious graduate school of education and had both a national and international network. I was off his list permanently, and it was a major personal loss. Having learned the hard way, I suggest you take great care to avoid an eleventh-hour excuse for turning down a job offer.

Salary

It is not unusual for a candidate to be involved in a search where the compensation, which includes salary and benefits, is not determined until the end of the process. This is especially true in superintendent searches and also in the case of administrative candidates in general. Or, if compensation is stated, the notice may read "depending upon experience and qualifications." Frequently, candidates do not want to ask what the total compensation is for fear of being disqualified early in the process for being "interested in money and not the job." If money is your primary consideration, this probably is a job you do not want anyway. If so, move along.

All candidates have the right to inquire, early in the job hunt, what the approximate compensation will be. There is little reason to remain in a search if the compensation is not to your liking. If, however, you are in need of employment, the compensation level may not play a major role in your decision. In the case of teachers, it is fairly easy to establish the salary because it is determined on the basis of a grid. Placement on the grid is usually a function of years of experience and level of education. For administrators it is more difficult, but not impossible, to determine what the compensation will be.

The reason for knowing what the compensation level is at the outset of the search is to avoid dropping out at the last minute when you finally learn that what is being offered is unacceptable and far from the higher figure you had in mind. You want to avoid withdrawing at the end of the process because of information you failed to acquire at the beginning of the search.

The Commute

I have had candidates withdraw late in the process because they "discovered" that the commute was too difficult. I rarely worked with these candidates a second time. Determining whether the commute is acceptable or not is a factor that should have been explored before an application was submitted. The use of this excuse is unacceptable to a consultant and employer. Often, to distance himself from this decision, an applicant will place the blame on his spouse, stating that the commute is too long and will keep him away from family for unacceptable periods of time. When applying for a position, you must travel the round trip to the potential work site during the same hours of the day and night you would normally travel to work or associated meetings. In order to accurately determine driving times, avoid conducting your travel research during popular vacation periods or the summer months.

Family Concerns

Immediate family considerations are important and need to be factored into the decision-making process. We know from experience, in both the private and public arenas, that if the spouse or children are not happy with a physical move associated with a new job, it is more than likely that the candidate will not function at top efficiency on the job. The problem occurs when the candidate is offered a job and then refuses it because of family concerns. Like so many of the other early mistakes, this decision should be made at the beginning of the search, not at the end.

A candidate owes it to her family members to involve them early in the process so that there are no surprises. While it is common to involve one's spouse at the outset of the search, that is not always the case with children. Teenagers, in particular, have a major stake in any physical move a family makes. Your children have only one chance to attend school, and it needs to be a successful one. You will have other opportunities to pursue a professional move.

Health of Parents

Most experienced superintendent candidates are of the age where their parents are considered "elderly," whatever that means. Often, parents are not in the best of health, some clearly in poor health such that there is concern over their being able to care for themselves. Several finalists for top positions have backed away from job offers because they felt the need to be in the immediate geographic area where their parents live in case the latter need assistance. It is understandable that candidates would be so considerate of parents that they would forgo a professional move. Again, the issue is timing. Unless there has been an unexpected decline in the health of parents, the candidate should have considered this variable early in the search.

Real Estate Values, Equity in Property, and Moving Expenses

When you take a new position, it should be with the expectation that there is a gain in real income, taking into consideration the new cost of housing, travel, and moving costs, plus all of the expenses related to establishing a new household. Not to be forgotten in all of this is the value of fringe benefits you currently possess versus what you will receive. You need to be "made whole." I strongly suggest that you develop a financial plan that carefully compares all economic aspects of a move. Using the services of a financial planner is advisable.

So what is the mistake you may make? Simply that you commit to a position without a financial plan or that, once offered a position, you withdraw because you realize you made a serious economic mistake because of your failure to engage in an early due-diligence effort. The most important aspects of due diligence are related both to total compensation and to the dramatic differences in the price of housing in various regions of the country. Although you may move from a high-rent district to a poorer one, that is unlikely. Simply to move from one house to another in the same community usually costs more. What is more likely to happen is that someone moving up the career ladder will be moving to a more affluent community where the price of housing is higher.

A candidate must take the time at the front end of the job search to determine the burden that a new mortgage and associated moving expenses will place on new income. Small items may carry significant costs, such as those associated with new carpeting, drapes, and other household needs. All of these items are funded with after-tax dollars.

Spousal Job Dislocation

The public sector is unlike the private sector in many ways, one of which is the inability of a local governmental entity, such as a board of education, to hire one spouse and guarantee the other spouse employment in the district. And, when it is done, it can be perceived as a dangerous act of nepotism.

I am reminded of a superintendent candidate in another part of the country where there was some latitude in hiring a spouse in the same district. It was a very large school system. He was superintendent and his wife was a building principal, although he was hired first and he later hired his wife. At her time of hiring, he was instrumental in determining where she was placed on the administrative pay scale. Initially the placement was not questioned. However, after a state law enforcement official accused him of a serious financial wrongdoing, his wife's place-ment on the scale came under scrutiny both by his critics and support-ers. Although he was not forced from the district because of the salary placement, it provided another reason for critics to distrust him. He was later ousted from his position. The point is, do not plan on your spouse being employed in the same district where you may have influence or decision-making authority regarding the hiring of new employees. If you make a move, however, you need to give serious consideration to your spouse's employment.

A number of candidates ultimately turn down positions because spouses hold equally important and well-paying positions and are un-willing to relinquish them. Years ago it was not uncommon for men to take on new positions and expect their wives to simply pick up and fol-low them. That is no longer the case. Women are entering the educa-tional administrative ranks in numbers that are outpacing men. But, whatever the case, it cannot be expected that a spouse, male or female, will automatically give up a position to be with the other partner.

The issue at play is similar to those that have been described through-out this section. You and your spouse need to make a decision well be-fore the process gets serious as to whether one spouse is willing to fol-low the other or whether both of you stay where you are for now.

Pension Benefits and Concerns

There is no aspect of relocating that presents as many serious issues as the matter of a pension. And there is no excuse more abused than the one dealing with the pension issue.

Efforts to coordinate pension plans from state to state have proved fruitless. Years ago, a major effort was made by a high-powered com-mission to coordinate the pension plans of the six New England states in an attempt to ease the movement of educators among the states. In spite of an extensive effort, there was little progress. What is not gener-ally considered is that pension plans are big businesses in each state. They can be a source of reserve funds for state officials to borrow from to temporarily eliminate deficit gaps in other accounts. The huge size of pension funds provides opportunities for powerful state officials to ap-point financial advisors who collect substantial fees. The funds are subject to political maneuvering and are overseen by powerful state teacher associations. Any effort to equalize pension benefits or contributions to the system would result in some states having to fund large increases in pension benefits. It is a given that a unified program would have to reflect the state program that is the most generous of those included in the new system. This will not happen. That said, candidates have to live with pension systems as they exist.

Because of the significant differences in pension benefits, state to state, and the factors that determine benefits, candidates need to take great care before relocating to another state. For the vast majority of educators, state pension benefits are the major source of retirement income. It is vital that a careful analysis be made of the benefits you are able to accumulate in the state from which you are moving as compared to the benefits to be received in the new state. Vesting periods vary greatly and conditions that govern reenrolling in a plan if you return to your home state are complicated matters. Small nuances can have a great impact. If ever there is a time for expert assistance, it is when you are dealing with pension issues.

There are thousands of educators who, because of their inability to maintain a professional position in one state for very long, have accumulated time in a number of states but are unable to retire with a decent pension from any of them. Over the years, I have worked with dozens of candidates who have dropped out of a search at the last minute once they discovered the downside of leaving one pension system for another. Unlike the other excuses for refusing a job offer, this one straddles my entire history in education. The gravity of the issue never changes, only the candidates do.

The lesson to be learned is that you must not wait until the end of a search to explore pension systems and the impact they will have on your retirement income. This is a case where due diligence must be undertaken early in the search. Do not rely on either the consultant or employer to provide valuable advice. They are not experts in pension matters. Employ a pension expert. Better yet, ask the new district at the time it is getting serious about your candidacy if it is willing to fund the hiring of a pension specialist.

The next step in the job-hunt process is for you to become a detective and learn about the new district and those who work there.

8

HOLMES AND WATSON, FRONT AND CENTER

Long before you enter the interviewing room, you need to prepare for your entrance. This stage of the search will test your investigative skills. It is vital that you gather information that will help you conduct a great interview and then assist you in making a sound decision, if offered the position. All too often, candidates enter a search without ever having researched the answers to essential questions or without having collected essential data. There is little sense in entering a job hunt if you are not convinced that it is the right position for you. Better that you exit early rather than be disappointed later. A job search, if properly conducted, is stressful and time consuming. If you enter it seriously, do so on the basis of good information. Now is the time to highlight your inquisitive nature, to engage in real-time snooping, to put away the crystal ball, and work with your magnifying glass. If you have ever dreamed about being an amateur sleuth, this is your chance.

ASSESS THE PROSPECTIVE DISTRICT

The more you learn about a district, the less likely you are to make a poor decision. I have had candidates drop out of the competition in what appeared to be outstanding districts because they did not view the position in a positive light after collecting relevant data. Information can be acquired from:

- Websites of local and metropolitan newspapers that cover the district
- Visits to the community to determine if this is the district in which you want to work
- Professional contacts with educators in the district or with someone who knows them
- Print materials about the district from websites or the district office
- The district's website for timely information on ongoing activities
- Minutes of the governing board's meetings
- State department of education website for district information
- A review of all standardized test score data for the district
- The executive director of state professional associations
- Personal contacts who may have additional information

ANALYZE THE POSITION

Although the preceding list provides good sources of information, it deals primarily with collecting objective data. The following list, if used, will provide valuable information on relationships within the district at all levels of the organization.

If you are a superintendent, the reputation of the board is essential to your decision. I have had candidates drop out of searches because the more they learned about a governing board, the more convinced they were that there would be efforts by the board to micromanage their work. This is especially true for superintendent candidates. Other qualified candidates will not apply in some districts for the same reason. Candidates for principal positions have a similar responsibility to themselves to determine the leadership style of the superintendent since it may be a style that certain principals may not be comfortable working with.

For whatever position you apply, it is wise to review this list for those considerations that will impact your success in a district. While comparative data is important to your decision, your success in the new district will be determined in great measure by successful interpersonal relationships.

- Does the job description match your professional needs?
- Is it a new position, a downsized position, or a reconstituted position?
- Was a former employee pushed out of the position?
- Is the position being created to solve a problem, and if so, what problem?
- To whom would you report?
- Who would you be supervising and evaluating?
- Is it a growth position?
- What is the reputation of your immediate supervisor?
- What is the reputation of the district?
- What is the reputation of the superintendent?
- What is the reputation of the governing board?
- Compare your strengths with the district's needs.
  - Identify your leadership style if you are seeking an administrative position.
  - Determine if your leadership style is compatible with that of your new supervisor.
  - List your strengths and shortcomings.
  - Match your strengths against the job description.
  - Determine if your shortcomings will present a problem for you.
- Is the total compensation package adequate?
- Are you convinced you can be successful in the position?
- Will you accept the position if offered?

INSIDE CANDIDATES

If you arrive at the stage where you are convinced by all of the measures noted above that you are ready to proceed, there is a final issue to be addressed: that of inside candidates. Of all the background data you collect, this may be the most important. You need to determine if there is an inside candidate. If the person in charge of the search is unwilling to provide an answer, then that refusal may be your answer.

One of the most difficult aspects of a search for a consultant to get across to a candidate is the notion that at times it is best not to enter a search if there is a well-respected inside candidate. There are many reasons why a district will announce a search knowing full well that it wants the inside candidate. I recall vividly being interviewed several times as a superintendent search consultant in districts where there was the expectation that there would be a strong inside candidate. At all of the meetings I have with board members, the question is invariably raised as to how I, as the consultant, treat inside candidates. My answer has always been the same: I treat them as I do anyone else. There will be occasions when inside candidates are successful in being selected by me to be in the finals, and there will be other times when they are not selected. But what I also share with the hiring district is that if there's a strong inside candidate who appears to have significant support on the board and who is likely to be appointed to the position, then do not conduct a search. Outside candidates will view the search as a sham. Such a search discredits the district, the consultant, and the insider who receives the appointment. Do your homework and then decide whether you have any chance to succeed against an insider.

IMPLEMENTING WHAT YOU HAVE LEARNED

Experience tells me that not all of what you will learn through your research will be important to know in all of your searches. Eventually, however, most of what you learned will be of some use. You need to constantly remind yourself that the goal is to distance yourself from all other candidates for the position.

Once you feel confident that you have done what needs to be done before the interview, you must still continue your preparation. The following chapter describes in detail both appropriate and inappropriate grooming.

⑨

DRESS BRITISH

From the outset of my consultant work, I have made a point to inform candidates that good grooming will not be the reason they secure a job, but poor grooming will weigh heavily against them. Ten years later, this advice still holds true. I never cease to be amazed at the carelessness of candidates when it comes to dress and grooming for an interview. An outstanding superintendent friend of mine once shared with me the thought, "If you want to impress anyone at all, dress British."

PORTRAIT OF A CANDIDATE

It is said that a picture is worth a thousand words. Therefore, I will share portraits of three candidates, each of which depicts the worst-case scenario about dress and grooming. In all three cases there were happy endings, two of which would not have occurred without our direct intervention. In the third case, the candidate acquired a new position in a less-desirable district. She at least had the opportunity to relocate and get a fresh start. We never had the opportunity to consult with her after our first experience, so we do not know whether anyone gave her the advice she needed.

Candidate Number One

I'll call the first job-hunt candidate Michael. We first met him while conducting a search in his district for a new superintendent. The district was high profile, prestigious, wealthy, and one where students performed exceptionally well. It was a highly respected district in the state in which it is located. The then-current superintendent and board worked out a mutually satisfactory and civil separation. The board had lost confidence in her and she, in turn, believed strongly that the board was constantly micromanaging her. Most likely the truth was somewhere in between. It was time for a separation, one that would eventually prove of benefit to both parties.

Michael held a high-ranking central office position in this district, one that required him to be something of a hatchet man for the superintendent and board. Consequently, he had created a somewhat fearsome reputation with the staff (especially the teacher union) because he was the one who, during severe budget reductions, had to make significant staff cuts. For several reasons, the board was not interested in him as a candidate for the superintendent position and suggested to him privately that he not apply. He accepted the board's suggestion. As an important aside, the chair of the board asked me if one of the consultants in my firm could see fit to talk to Michael about his appearance. I agreed that we would do so at the appropriate time but not before the search was concluded.

In my opinion and especially in the mind of one of the other consultants, Michael was a talented administrator who had not been given an opportunity to succeed. Further, we believed that the superintendent should have spoken to Michael earlier in his career about the grooming issue but had failed to do so. Because of Michael's position, we worked with him closely in terms of the logistics of the search we were conducting in his district. The complexity of the search was such that there were four of us on site for portions of the search, and we sometimes kidded among ourselves about Michael having cornered the market on green polyester suits, unpolished shoes, thrift shop ties, and shirts with frayed collars. But, in spite of that kidding, one consultant saw him as brilliant, forthright, ethical, and of superintendent caliber.

Michael came to trust the consultant and after the search was concluded, he took it upon himself to ask if we would provide him professional advice in terms of applying for superintendent positions. This provided an opportunity for one of the consultants, a female, to offer him some frank advice. Eager to move his career along, he was secure enough to seek help and she offered it.

She sent him on a shopping trip to an upscale, conservative shop in the city to purchase a dark blue "interviewing" suit. She also recommended a straight collar shirt, dress shoes, and an expensive tie. She conferred with him about grooming. She made specific suggestions and he accepted them. Shortly after that, we put him into a search in a very powerful district. He was the hands-down choice, carrying himself with confidence during the entire process, but especially during the personal interview. He looked every inch the confident, powerful, intelligent, and capable person that he was.

Did he get this appointment because of his dress and general grooming? I do not know about that, but I do know he would not have been in the search if he were still in his green polyester suit. All along, I have said that good grooming will not get you a job, but poor grooming will certainly be a factor if you do not get it. I think Michael is somewhat of an exception to this philosophy. He assumed an air of confidence that resulted in large measure because others responded to him differently from when he was that poorly groomed educator to whom no one gave a second glance.

His wife had the most poignant observation when Michael returned from picking up his new clothes and trying them on for her before the first board interview. She spoke with the consultant with whom Michael had worked on the grooming issue. She shared with the consultant that she had forgotten how attractive her husband was. She said that during their married life he mostly thought about her and the children and simply did not spend much on clothing for himself. Having been around educators my entire career, this is a story that can often be heard. It is caused in part by simply not having the financial means to do what is necessary. It paid for Michael to dress British.

If there is a moral to this case, it is that supervisors need to help subordinates by being forthright about matters of dress and grooming. It is a difficult task to tell someone that she dresses poorly or that he needs to pay more attention to personal grooming, yet this is a task that has to be undertaken.

Candidate Number Two

This is a case of a female candidate for a superintendent position. Let us call her Alice. She had been employed in a rural district in one of the northern New England states as a superintendent. Things had not gone as well as she wanted during her tenure there; it had been her first superintendent position, and she had little staff support and no prior mentoring to speak of. Alice had subsequently taken a position overseas as a curriculum director in a very large district as a way to recycle her career. Although her work overseas was outstanding, she wanted to return to New England.

She submitted excellent papers and, as a result, I scheduled an interview. She was a bright and talented candidate. I was impressed with her understanding of curriculum, an area of great importance to the district where she had applied. The interview itself went well—but there was the matter of dress. At best, I would describe it as inappropriate, even a bit provocative. Yet I did not believe Alice perceived it that way. The facts were that everything was too tight, too short, and too garish. Not a very professional picture. Yet Alice was clearly a talented educator, and I wanted to provide her an opportunity to compete. She also possessed high-level interpersonal skills, a quality I thought a staff in a small district would respond to positively. I invited her to the board interview— but not without first dealing with the matter of dress. This being my first meeting with her, it was a bit awkward, but I owed it to her to address it. I did so as delicately as I could, and she received it well. Unfortunately, I had forgotten to discuss the appropriate use of perfume and regretted it as the search progressed.

The interview with the board took place on a brutally hot, stifling July night. The school was closed for summer maintenance and had the look and feel of an old, tired body waiting for reconstructive surgery. The only room available for the interview was the teacher lounge, which was next to the cafeteria. The stale smell of a closed-up cafeteria waiting to be cleaned eased its way into the lounge. Coupled with the heat, it was an unbearable setting. There was no air conditioning, and the temperature outside was higher than that inside. Opening windows served no useful purpose as we soon learned. The air felt wet from the high humidity. It was an August "dog day" in July.

Present were nine members of the board plus the candidate and myself. I met Alice in the main office and immediately knew I had a problem. While her dress was acceptable, she had on perfume that sold in bulk and she had used a considerable dosage for this interview! I had no choice but to forge ahead with the interview. I introduced her to the members of the board and the perfume immediately penetrated the air. We were but a few minutes into the interview when, in desperation, board members started to throw open windows, while others excused themselves to use the restrooms. But, with the outside temperature at least equal to the inside temperature, there was no relief and the interview was a short-lived struggle.

I called Alice the next day and addressed the issue of the perfume and her grooming. This type of conversation is never easy, but it is necessary. The end of this story is that she took the advice professionally and did acquire a position as superintendent in northern New England. In retrospect, perhaps I should not have moved her along initially, yet there was much about her that was positive.

The two cases illustrate the importance of good grooming. In the first case, the consultant built confidence in Michael by telling him he was qualified to be a superintendent, but that he was destroying his chances because he failed to present himself as a successful CEO. It was the confidence building that was so important. If he had not improved his grooming, I would not have promoted him as a candidate in this particular upscale district. Although he possessed the talent to be a superintendent, it would have had to be in a district where appearances did not count.

In the second case, the limited advice I initially offered did not work because Alice was out of her element. I failed to give her the help she needed beforehand. Yet, her unsuccessful interview with the board afforded me the opportunity to speak honestly with her about her grooming. The story ended happily in that she acquired a position in her home state.

Candidate Number Three

I interviewed this candidate for a position in another state, in an outstanding district where the governing board sets the standard for professional conduct. It was also a district where members of the community were involved and played an important and participatory role in the search process. The entire search was flawless due in large measure to the attitude of the board and community committees.

The candidate was a superintendent but was being nonrenewed in her current district. The reason for nonrenewal was not related to her ability but rather to her style of leadership, one that was no longer appropriate. Her current district was middle class whereas the district she was applying to was upper class. There was no reason to believe that she could not run the new district given her prior experience. It is worth noting that she was short of stature and a bit "chunky." Nevertheless, she was a professionally qualified candidate with many years of successful experience. It was only recently that a strain had developed between her and the board.

The nature of this search was such that there was a twenty-six-member interviewing committee comprised mostly of community persons and a lesser number of staff. Board members were only observers at the session. The interview took place on a hot Saturday in May. It was held in a large meeting room in one of the schools. The room was set up in a large U-shape using typical cafeteria-type tables. When a candidate entered the room to be interviewed, he or she entered at the open end of the U and then proceeded to walk around the inside of the U to greet and be greeted by each interviewer. The table at which the candidate sat was situated by itself at the open end of the U-shaped table arrangement. None of the tables, including the one at which the candidate sat, had vanity skirts.

I met the candidate at the entrance to the school and introduced her to the chair of the interviewing committee. I knew then that this was not going to be a good day. She wore a skirt that was unusually short. The minute she entered the room, there was a quiet gasp, however polite. The interview itself went well except that without a vanity skirt in front of the table, there were moments of silent embarrassment. This was a case of talent wasted because of indiscreet grooming. I did not have an opportunity to represent her again, but I do know that she was hired in another district with demographics much like the district she was leaving. She did not ask for feedback, and I offered none at that time but would have if she had applied for another position for which I was the search consultant. I was surprised that this candidate, given her years of experience, failed to understand appropriate grooming protocols. Did indiscreet grooming cost her the job? In and of itself, probably not. But it certainly distracted from her overall presentation.

PERSONAL GROOMING

Protocols

Grooming for an interview in education is somewhat different from in many other professions. Education is a very conservative occupation. Most teachers and administrators dress conservatively. Most of what educators wear is off the rack. Unlike the dot.com industry where casual dress is the order of the day, educators never veer very far from the conservative norm. Much has been written about appropriate dress codes in the private sector. Colors and styles change with the times. First, it was dark blue suits to project a presidential image, and then it was gray to suggest rock-solid dependability and long-term commitment. I remember when it was in vogue to wear Jerry Garcia ties with bright vivid colors, and then it was the Regis Philbin look with the color-coordinated shirt and tie. But, whatever it is, you need to make it conservative to be successful and to be accepted in educational circles.

Based on hundreds of interviews I conducted and from watching the reaction of hundreds of other interviewers, the following are considered acceptable grooming norms:

1. Consider the season, time of day the interview is being held, location of interview, and the audience, and then plan accordingly. Do not wait until the last minute to decide what you will wear. Thought needs to be given to several factors. For example, if the interview is during the summer and scheduled in the evening in a school building, you can safely assume that the air conditioning has been shut down for the summer. It is almost a certainty that the room will be hot and stuffy. Alternatively, if the interview is held in the central office, the chances are good that the building will be air-conditioned. This new location may allow you the opportunity to wear something different.

2. If you are traveling a long distance to an interview, take into consideration what impact sitting in a car, train, or plane for several hours will have on your appearance. For example, a button-down collar shirt will look rumpled and tired after a long trip. The suggestion is to not wear a button-down or, if the job is in a district where the preppy, conservative look is expected, then bring along another shirt.

3. Casual clothes are never acceptable unless you have been told to dress casually; even then, you need to be careful that you do not dress down too far. I once invited a candidate to come casual to an interview since it was a Saturday morning and only the two of us would be present. He arrived unshaven and wearing a tank top and dirty jeans. That was the last time I advised someone to dress down for any level of interview.

4. The first items of clothing interviewers generally notice with men are shirt, collar, and tie. Once into the interview, it is the suit. As they exit, it is often the shoes. For women, the first thing noticed is an overall impression and then length of skirt. Once the interview is underway, the next things noticed in terms of grooming are use of jewelry and perfume.

5. Dark suits are always the norm both for men and women, although during the warm months, women are able to wear lighter-colored clothing and make a nice appearance. For men, there is no alternative to business suits on the dark side. The rule of thumb is that you cannot go wrong with a conservative dark suit, skirt, or pantsuit. One of my more recent searches had several women as candidates, three of whom became semifinalists. Two of them I knew professionally as fellow superintendents. The other, from the Midwest, I had not met until she applied for this search, although we had had two telephone interviews. When the candidate from the Midwest left the room and an assessment of her interview began, one board member, instead of weighing the candidate's qualifications, referred to her as "looking too matronly." The board did not move her forward.

6. Shirt collars for men present an interesting dilemma. Most educators are prone to wearing shirts with button-down collars. As mentioned, shirts with button down collars look appropriate if fresh

looking, but they do not hold up well under travel. For that reason, I suggest a straight collar with stays. They always look fresh.

7. The inappropriate use of cologne and perfume has, in my experience, lost jobs for otherwise qualified candidates. It is not a serious issue for men since few wear cologne, and those who do wear cologne seem to be discreet in its use. But, to my surprise, many women overuse perfume. In close quarters, where most interviews are held, it can be a major distraction.

8. Jewelry must be worn with discretion. I was present at a board interview with a very experienced high school principal candidate. He lost the support of one of the major players in the interview because of his use of jewelry. The candidate failed to assess the culture of the community where he applied. Women need to be especially careful not to flaunt expensive jewelry and diamonds since they run the risk of offending interviewers with their display of wealth.

9. Haircuts are occasionally a problem with women but for the most part they seem to know the right thing to do. Those who do have a problem tend to have long hair that is combed or cut so that it falls over one eye. When this is the case they have the distractive motion of continuously tossing their head to get the hair out of their eyes. Men in general have improved in their grooming but occasionally a candidate will be beyond the date he should have had a haircut. Some men are very careless about letting hair grow out of nose and ears. This is unacceptable grooming. The impression it leaves is that the candidate is old and careless.

10. Beards and mustaches continue to be a point of concern. Many men ask me what impact I think facial hair will have on the interview. My answer is always the same: if you can get through an interview without making the interviewers uncomfortable with your facial hair, it will have no impact. However, a friend of mine who counsels those in job hunts in private industry told me that if a candidate asks him if a mustache or beard will be a problem, he bluntly tells them to get rid of either or both. He takes the position that if candidates ask the question they are already sensitive to facial hair being an issue and it only serves to distract them from having a good interview.

Grooming Disasters

The following are portraits of men and women with whom I have worked and who violated the grooming protocols noted above.

1. Candidates no. 2 and no. 3 were described earlier and are perfect examples of how wearing indiscreet clothing and using perfume to excess led to their being eliminated quickly from the search process. They gave the respective boards no opportunity to discover what talents they possessed. This rule of thumb remains: if in doubt, dress conservatively, discreetly, and smartly. Another colleague, who has considerable experience with interviewing at the collegiate level, told me that he informs candidates that, when in doubt as to the grooming protocol, to "dress up." The point is that you will be less uncomfortable being overdressed for the interview than if you are dressed too casually. If you feel uncomfortable, you can always remove a tie or jacket.

2. I worked with an outstanding male superintendent who was at the time employed in a large urban district where he had been his entire career. He began as a teacher and worked his way to becoming superintendent. In addition to being talented, he was the perfect gentleman, intelligent, a prodigious worker, and very successful. On three different occasions he was a finalist for a superintendent position. He lived a significant driving distance from the location of the three job opportunities. As a result of the distance, I strongly suggested to him that he should arrive the night before in order to be rested for the interviews. As an important aside, his national heritage was such that his complexion was normally sallow and, when tired, he acquired a slightly jaundiced look. Fatigue resulted in his having deep, dark circles under his eyes. Still, he was an exceptional candidate. His fault was his stubbornness in not making arrangements that would allow him to appear for an interview looking rested and energized. Instead, with several hours of travel behind him, he arrived exhausted and rumpled looking. He looked far older than his years and gave the impression he did not have the energy to deal with the demands of the position. He had ignored my suggestion and instead drove approx-

imately ten hours one way to each of the interviews. He was not offered any of the three positions.

3. In many of the northeastern states, there is an expectation that
conservative suits are the norm. However, not all sections of the
nation share that view. Much has to do with climate, temperature,
and regional culture. However, "when in Rome do as the Romans
do" needs to be the standard. I worked with a candidate from another part of the country whose dress covered all bases. At his first
interview with the board he arrived in a green sports jacket with
gold buttons, and casual slacks. He definitely reinforced the fact
that he was from a warmer climate and at least one board member
mentioned this after the interview. At the second interview he arrived in a very light blue suit with a purplish tie. After that interview another board member observed that the candidate looked as
though he came from Los Angeles. For the third interview, he
wore a blue blazer with a white shirt and blue collar. The comment
was made that he looked like he was from Manhattan. (It is worth
noting that everything he wore to the interviews was expensive.)
Finally, after the third interview, when it was clear to me that he
was a front-runner, a couple of board members questioned
whether or not he would fit in culturally, a comment that was mo-
tivated by the candidate's dress. At that point, I spoke with the candidate and suggested that a more conservative look would be helpful. He arrived for the final round in a gray flannel suit! Of course,
gray flannel has been out of vogue for some time, but it nevertheless was viewed as more in keeping with northeast educational culture. He was appointed superintendent.

4. I recommended a high school principal who was then working in a
large district for a parallel position in a small, professionally attractive Hartford, Connecticut, suburb. When I first met him I
knew he was more avant-garde than my usual high school principal candidate. He was more "big city" in manner and dress than
most conservative New England principals. However, he had the
professional qualifications to be successful in the new position. I
had mentioned to him during our initial interview that he was
competing for a position in a conservative community and he
should dress and act accordingly. He arrived in a dark suit, black

turtleneck, and a large gold medallion hanging from his neck. Added to that look was a large and expensive-looking gold Rolex watch. He looked big city when he needed to play a small-town role. The most senior and influential member of the board took an immediate dislike to the candidate's gold medallion, black turtleneck, and Rolex watch. Then the board member, convinced that this candidate was not going forward in the search, decided to test the integrity of the candidate by asking a question that he raised with each candidate. The board member asked the candidate the name of the most recent book he had read. The candidate responded with a title and author. The board member then focused in on the book, and it soon became evident that the candidate had not read the book but, at best, had scanned a review. Unfortunately for the candidate, the interviewer had read the book. Between the dress and the book, the candidate was eliminated.

5. I had been working on an organizational study and, in the course of my work, met the principal of the school. Since she was included in the data gathering for the study due to her administrative position, I had occasion to confer with her several times. She seemed perfectly suited to her role as principal and appeared to have promise as an administrator. A year or so later, I was conducting a search for an elementary school principal and she applied. Because I knew her from my working on the organizational study in her district, I did not bother to interview her formally and scheduled her to meet with the interview committee, a meeting at which I was present. She arrived wearing a ring on every finger and both thumbs. Because I was sitting at the opposite end of a long table, I did not get an exact count, but she wore a minimum of fifteen bracelets on one wrist and several more on her other wrist. While this is an exception to how most women present themselves, it is, nevertheless, a factual account and gives credence to the fact that there are candidates who simply have no sense as to what appropriate grooming means.

6. My most memorable facial hair story had a happy ending, but it also answers the question as to what impact facial hair has on an interview. This was a candidate with whom I had worked earlier in his career. I knew him to be outstanding at his work as superin-

tendent. He was interested in a professional change, and I placed him into a new set of interviews. Like many other men with facial hair, he was curious as to the effect it would have. I like to think it has no impact. He almost proved me wrong. I scheduled him for the first of two interviews with the board. Self-conscious about his mustache and trying hard not to scratch at it, as is often the case with mustached men, he instead would quickly rub at it with one of his knuckles. He did this quickly, thinking the faster he did it, the less apt we would be to notice it. Confident he would get through this first interview, I wanted to share with him before the next interview the impression he was leaving as it concerned his mustache. I decided to count the number of times he rubbed at the mustache. He did so approximately every forty-five seconds or, in the course of an hour interview, eighty times! It was not long before interviewers lost interest in what is being said and began to focus on the mustache. Perhaps my friend's approach, suggested previously, is the better one. If the candidate is worried enough to ask about facial hair, maybe it should be removed.

Two Additional Grooming Success Stories

For all the mistakes candidates make with grooming, there are many examples of outstanding grooming. The two candidates described below demonstrate how appropriate grooming gets you through the first step of job search. I worked with both candidates and both were appointed superintendents. There are many other success stories, but these two stories highlight many important points for candidates in the job hunt.

The first portrait paints a picture of an educator who was an assistant superintendent at the time of her interview. Out of seven candidates I recommended to the board, the male chair indicated to me early in the process that in his opinion this candidate was running last. Questioning why I had her in the pool at all, I told him that her academic credentials were outstanding and that she brought appropriate experiences as an elementary principal and assistant superintendent. She had worked in communities where success was not easy to acquire but she had done so with distinction. Her references were excellent. In short, she was a terrific candidate. At this early stage of the search, I considered her the best qualified for the position but, in keeping with the firm's philosophy, did not share my opinion with the client. In fact, she was eventually appointed to the position.

Was her outstanding grooming the reason? It is difficult to tell, but I do know that whenever she stepped into the room she had an immediate positive impact on interviewers. The first time we met this candidate it was during a screening interview at which two consultants were present. From that first engagement, it was clear that she had a sophisticated sense of good grooming. It is worth noting that at the time of this search the candidate was the youngest person we had worked with on a superintendent search. I distinctly remember her telling us that before an interview she would have her mom critique the outfit she planned on wearing to an interview. Her mom obviously had good taste. The care the candidate took in her grooming and dress showed in her overall presence. She stayed with the fundamental rules of a dark business suit, silk blouse, skirt of appropriate length, minimal use of perfume, and limited use of cosmetics and jewelry. Overall, she presented a classic New England conservative educator look.

The second portrait is that of an out-of-state candidate who was competing with many in-state superintendents. He was an excellent superintendent, articulate, bright, and thoroughly qualified. Physically he was of small stature, reserved, and not prone to be assertive in an interview. His strengths, as he saw them and as I saw them, were his knowledge of education and the experience he could bring to a new position. He was an educator of proven integrity.

I had known him for several years at the time of his wanting to return to the state. We met and I made two suggestions to him. First, I believed that there was a need for him to take command of the interview, and I demonstrated how to do this. Up until this point, he was always reacting to the interviewers and did not demonstrate the energy and assertiveness they were usually looking for. A good student, he listened and responded positively to the suggestion. Second, there was the question of what he wore. He has a very fair complexion, and coupled with his slight physical stature, he came across as almost too youthful and gave little sense of command in spite of the fact that he was a proven leader. However, if he did not get past the interview, there would be no site visit that would provide the opportunity to prove his ability. Each time we met, he wore tan or brown suits regardless of the season. With this color, he just about faded into the background. He shifted to a dark blue suit, and assumed a more commanding presence at interviews. He was successful his next time out and secured a superintendent position in the state. Again, was it the change of color that caused him to succeed? All I know is that when I monitored the interviews that led to his successful job search, I witnessed a more confident educator who created an image of being capable and in-charge. Much like the female candidate described above, this male candidate also possessed a classic look in terms of dress and grooming.

My experience is that "clothes make the man (and woman)." Dress British and prepare for your dress rehearsal, the subject of chapter 10.

⑩

DRESS REHEARSAL

If you made it this far without deciding to make a strategic withdrawal and wait for another day to compete, you have demonstrated the perseverance needed to succeed in the interview. Before you meet the interviewers, however, there is a need to review important points. Just as the actress runs through a dress rehearsal to get her lines and movements down pat, you also need to make one last review before stepping onto the stage.

PREPARING FOR SHOW TIME AND THE UNEXPECTED

To begin with, you need to look at your situation much like an actor who has a different engagement every night in a different town. You can never be certain what the setting will be where you have to perform, what the audience will be like, and what other impediments or unexpected factors will come into play. In the actor's case, he could be performing before an audience of quiet, conservative seniors or before an ill-mannered, rowdy crowd of conventioneers. Whatever the situation, the show must go on. You must be prepared for the worst-case scenario since not all interviewing committees know exactly how to stage a good interview. Not all interviewers are polite or capable.

In seeking search consultant work, I have been interviewed by committees of two and committees of twenty-two. Interviews have taken place in cafeterias, teacher lounges, boardrooms, town hall meeting rooms, auditoriums, classrooms, country clubs, and yacht clubs. I have been interviewed behind closed doors and before television audiences. There have been interviewers who were cordial and others who were discourteous. There were those I sensed as being open-minded and others who already had another consultant in mind. Some interviewing sites were accommodating while others were pitifully inadequate. You never know what to expect. Therefore, be prepared for whatever turns up and get on with it.

NINETEEN STEPS TO PRACTICE DURING REHEARSAL

1. You should arrive in the community early and locate the building where the interviews are to be held. You may even want to locate the room, but under no circumstances are you to disturb the ongoing interviews. Once you have located the room, find another location to wait for your appointment. Rarely will provisions have been made to entertain you while you wait. If you are early, it is a good time to sit in your car and reflect on the job and the points you want to leave with the interviewers. I usually sought out a coffee shop or restaurant to fill in the time. It is a good time to review whatever data your research yielded.

2. You should not bring any documents into the room unless requested by the interview committee. Leave your portfolio, briefcase, travel bag, and oversized purse at home. Put nothing on the table. Keep a clear line of sight with everyone. Over the years, I have witnessed many interviews in which candidates have hauled large quantities of documents into the interviewing room that were never used. Do not bring bottled water with you; the interview is not taking place in the desert. And do not distribute handouts because that activity will change the flow of the interview. At this stage in the process, you should have sent all required materials. If you need to bring something into the room as a security blanket, try a 3 × 5-inch index card and a pen to jot

down whatever it is you think you want to remember. Beyond that, bring nothing.

3. You should have conducted your own research about the position and district. Never depend solely on data received from others. Using outdated or inaccurate information will usually work to your disadvantage. Remember that other candidates are doing their best to move ahead of you in terms of impressing the interviewers. Chapter 8, "Holmes and Watson, Front and Center," provides detailed guidelines for analyzing and gathering information.

4. Be prepared for the obvious questions that have to do with your areas of expertise and with the district's expectations for this position. Administrators can expect to be queried about test scores, full inclusion, dealing with marginal teachers, discipline, "pushy" parents, and similar topics. You should have no difficulty in preparing for these questions. If you know your business, the answer to this type of question amounts to nothing more than articulating it. You have to prepare for the less obvious question you may not have thought about. What books have you read recently? Who is your favorite educator? Why are you here? What makes you think you are ready for this position? It will be the confidence with which you answer these questions that will leave a lasting impression, not simply the answers.

5. Do not engage in gimmickry. Do not wear an "I love kids" button. No flowers in the lapel. Keep the Snoopy ties in the closet. And leave your portfolio at home unless it was requested. Bring nothing with you into the room except your wits, your commitment, your energy, and the real you. At one of our interviews, a "big city" superintendent was being interviewed in an upscale district. He arrived with a huge portfolio case that I associate with art students who are carrying samples of their work to be displayed to the interviewer. Asked to touch on the highlights of his career, he whipped open the case, complete with a portable easel, and spent half of his allotted interview time throwing chart after chart on the easel and reading the material to the interviewers. The governing board did not grant him a second interview.

6. You should always assume that the competition will be tough, whether true or not. Although you want to anticipate what the

competition may be doing, you also need to remain true to what you believe. If, for example, you do not believe in social promotion, then say so, but be certain you have defensible reasons and valid evidence that indicates most children profit by being retained. If you believe that full inclusion does a disservice to non–special-needs students, then say so but, once again, you must be armed with good data. Always keep in mind that it is risky to take a stand from which there is no way to make a strategic withdrawal. Think carefully before you respond.

7. It pays to stand in front of a mirror and view yourself as you believe the interviewers will see you. Is there a confident and articulate educator looking back at you? Or do you see a shrinking violet who commands little respect? Lack of confidence is easy to detect in candidates. This may be your only chance to impress the interviewers, and you do not want to let it slip from your grasp.

8. Practice some of what it is you want to say. Think about the answers to the obvious questions such as those relating to test scores or the well-publicized initiatives that have been undertaken in the district. Be prepared for that for which you can prepare. You do not want a rehearsed speech in response to anticipated questions, but there are some topics about which you can begin to frame ideas long before the interview begins.

9. Practice your response to "Tell us something about yourself." What is there about you that it is important to share with the interviewers? Can you do it in two minutes or less? Use this question to quickly distance yourself from the competition by being creative in what you say and how you say it.

10. If you already work in the district in which you are applying for a new position, do not assume and certainly do not act as though you have an insider advantage over other candidates. You are just another competitor and are expected to act like one. You must pretend you are applying for a position in the district next door and are expected to act here as you would there. Do not expect to be treated more favorably than other candidates, and do not let the interviewers assume you expect to be treated differently.

11. The most effective educational leaders are those who have mastered listening skills. You must practice this art by listening care-

fully to the entire question before you respond. This is not the time to be impetuous. If you begin to answer the question before it is completed, you may well end up answering the wrong question. Patience is a virtue. Interviewers are looking at you as the future leader of the district, school, or classroom. They will be observing your mannerisms to determine if they will impede your work in the district. If you fail to listen now, why would interviewers believe you would listen to anyone after you are hired?

12. Answer every question truthfully. If you do not know the answer, do not attempt to create one. Do not offer data if you are uncertain of its validity and reliability. For example, if in the course of discussing test scores, you are asked if you are aware of the downward trend in the district's math score, do not indicate you do if you do not. The fact that you failed to do your homework is bad enough, but do not add fuel to the fire by having interviewers distrust you.

13. Avoid being long winded. Answer the question asked and then stop. Once you have done that, do not think you have to answer the questions a second time just in case you thought no one understood your answers the first time. If there is a silence after you have answered a question, it does not mean it fell short of the mark. Often, the interviewers are waiting for one of their colleagues who is asleep at the wheel to ask the next question. If the interviewers have a problem understanding your answer, one of them will most likely ask for clarification.

14. Do not denigrate your current employer or supervisor. The walls have ears, not to mention that it is ethically wrong to do so and the interviewers will most likely give you a negative rating for criticizing others. This does not mean you cannot explain a difficult situation, but you must be discreet in doing so. Many of the interviewers have been in tight spots themselves so they will understand your reluctance to say too much.

15. Be prepared to meet poor interviewers and to experience a setting for interviewing that is poorly formatted. The interviewers and the chair of the committee may not be as well prepared as you are. If a consultant is involved in your search, he or she most likely would have briefed the committee members on interviewing protocols.

But even then, the interviewers may not follow the script. Like most human activities, interviews will vary from outstanding to pitiful.

16. This is not a life-or-death situation. The worst that can happen is that you will not get the appointment. No one wants to come in second but you will survive to compete another day. While it may not be a happy ending, you can make it a valuable ending by reflecting upon what occurred and where you collapsed in terms of the interview. Debriefing yourself is a valuable exercise and is covered in chapter 18, "Reflections."

17. I mentioned earlier that interviewing is a competitive activity. It is also an opportunity to demonstrate what you know, to let others see who you are, and to present your ideas and beliefs. It is a stage on which you can perform. If you prepare well and if you have confidence in your knowledge base, the interviewing experience can be exhilarating! Think of it as opening night and the opportunity to give the performance of your career.

18. The composition of both an interviewing committee and the governing board will most likely be broad based and representative of many different groups in the community. It is commonplace to have representatives from PTA or PTO, civic groups, district professional organizations, and general community groups. You must be on your guard that you do not denigrate any person or group. While you may have an opinion regarding one or more of the organizations or their representatives, this is not the time to express it. Be especially careful with PTA and PTO groups because they are usually the most vocal and, oftentimes, the most powerful in the community.

19. Finally, if you have a temporary disability such as a bad back or any condition that is physically draining and that makes you look ill, tired, or otherwise off your form, you should inform the consultant or the chair of the interviewing committee beforehand. It is best that the interviewers know from the outset that your disability is temporary. Once they have this information, they can eliminate it as a cause of concern.

These reminders are based on the experiences of many other candidates. There is much more to preparing for an interview than meets the eye. You will not be able to address all of these reminders for any one interview, but you will have a more effective interview if you pay attention to most of them. Once you have had the opportunity to participate in your first interview, most of these reminders and review items will fall into place. But never forget that your goal is to get the appointment the first time out. Therefore, a thorough study of these reminders will serve you well. A well-done dress rehearsal will prepare you for a great interview.

The lesson to be learned is: do not be discouraged and do not lose faith. Withdrawing from competition is not the answer. Reviewing and debriefing your interview with the help of others will eventually pay dividends.

A SECOND CHANCE

As superintendent, I was often in the position where I had to decide between two candidates of equal ability. It was always a difficult choice, especially having to inform the candidate who came in second. Yet, on numerous occasions, when another position became available in the same subject or grade, I would automatically go back to the runner-up. These follow-ups are referred to as "call backs." It is a common practice in education. Two or three years may have passed, but I would, nevertheless, track them down to offer a new position to them. Interviewers, especially superintendents and those responsible for hiring, remember outstanding candidates. Chapter 18, "Reflections," describes in detail how the callback system works. Now we move on to chapter 11 and a description of fatal mannerisms and how to avoid them.

THE SWORD OF DAMOCLES: MANNERISMS

Finally, your moment has arrived. The interview is scheduled. Lights, camera, action. The stage is set and the curtain is about to rise. This is your chance to step into the spotlight. The moment you have prepared for is here. No more studying, no more rehearsals, and no more data collecting and analysis.

This is your chance to bring everything into focus. Remember, this will not be your success story unless you love the idea of being at the interview, challenging the interviewers, and motivating them to query you on whatever topics are important to them. You must absolutely not allow them to conclude this interview until you have presented yourself as the best of all candidates. If you implement what you have learned to date, the job may be yours.

There is a need to discuss mannerisms and how they can derail an interview. Often they can be fatal to your chances of success. Figuratively speaking, mannerisms are the equivalent of a sword over your head, a sword that can behead the interviewee after the display of a single inappropriate mannerism during an interview.

A mannerism is defined as "a characteristic and often unconscious mode or peculiarity of action, bearing, or treatment." Further, it is an "exaggerated or affected adherence to a particular style or manner."

It is safe to say that we all exhibit mannerisms, some more distracting than the other. The issue is not that we have mannerisms, rather it is the types of mannerisms we exhibit and the degree to which others view them as impediments. Earlier, I gave the example of the candidate who rubbed his mustache approximately eighty times in a one-hour interview. Before long, we were all observing his annoying mannerism rather than listening to what he had to say. This is not to suggest that a mannerism will prevent you from getting a new position—but it may well interfere in acquiring the position you want in the district you want. Many of the candidates who are the subjects of the mannerisms described herein have gone on to other positions but most did not acquire the job they wanted. Simply put, other candidates interviewed more effectively because they did not have distracting mannerisms. You do not want the interviewers distracted from their goal of learning as much as possible about you in the short time allotted to do so.

The mannerisms outlined here were exhibited both by experienced and inexperienced candidates. I noted earlier that in many cases the most experienced candidates have not interviewed in years. Many are also too vain to seek help.

The higher up the hierarchy that candidates are positioned, the more apt they are to convince themselves that they "know everything about interviewing." In fact, experienced candidates are more prone to poor interviews than less-experienced candidates who set aside their pride and seek assistance.

TEN OF THE MOST FATAL MANNERISMS

1. *Looking at the ceiling and elsewhere when searching for an answer.* I have yet to see an answer written on the ceiling. Avoiding eye contact when answering a question sends negative messages. It may signal that you are timid, lack confidence, or have poor interpersonal skills. The interviewers may project from this mannerism that you may not be able to interact effectively with staff. Education is an occupation in which highly honed interpersonal skills are critical requirements of all leaders.

2. *Resting your chin in your hand.* It is not uncommon to see candidates place one elbow on the table and then rest their chins in their hands. As an occasional gesture, it might be acceptable in the right situation, but as a continuing mannerism it is not an effective tactic. It is a mannerism that also suggests a lack of enthusiasm. If you are too tired for the interview, you should not be there! This is not the place to demonstrate a lack of energy.

3. *Placing fingers in your mouth.* I know that it stretches the imagination to think that adults would revert to a childhood behavior, but it is done and done often. It is a nervous habit of which the candidate is unaware. The worst case I saw of this was with a recently retired administrator who had many years of successful experience. He was seeking a part-time position that would not interfere with the pension rights earned from his last position. It was a perfect transition opportunity. Not only did he continually place a couple of fingers in his mouth throughout most of the interview but he also held his chin in his hand at the same time. Unless someone is forthright enough to alert him to this mannerism, he will continue to engage in it and continue to look foolish.

4. *Picking at your face.* While I discussed candidates who scratch at or rub a beard or mustache, there are others who nervously pick at or scratch their faces. Again, it is a nervous mannerism that is distractive and tends to make listening to the candidate more difficult for the interviewers. It is intriguing how a professional educator can advance this far in a career and not have addressed this mannerism. Where were his colleagues? Where was her supervisor?

5. *Tugging at the hem of a skirt.* Earlier, I presented a dramatic example of how a short skirt contributed to a candidate's losing an opportunity to continue in the search in an outstanding district. While that was one of the pronounced exceptions to good grooming, tugging at a skirt hem is a common, annoying mannerism. Candidates need to think ahead as to where interviews will take place. The consultant knows this ahead of time and can be of assistance. Otherwise, you need to look at the worst-case scenario and assume there will be no vanity skirts on the tables. If a skirt is too short, then the candidate most likely will be tugging at her

hem during the entire session. It may be acceptable to you to embarrass yourself, but it is not appropriate to embarrass the interviewers.

6. *Tossing hair out your face.* This is mostly a female mannerism
   and usually occurs when the candidate has long hair. Interestingly
   enough, women usually take great care with hair. It is obvious
   that the vast majority, just prior to the interview, have had a new
   cut and styling. They almost always look professional. The problem arises when the style is such that one eye is covered with hair
   and the candidate constantly shakes her head to get the hair out
   of her face. In other situations, it may be an attractive move, but
   in an interviewing room it is annoying. This is an interview, not an
   audition!

7. *Looking over the top of reading glasses.* This is a common trap
   that many who wear reading glasses fall into. Although they can
   be reasonably certain that they will not be expected to read anything at the interview, they almost always wear reading glasses. In
   fact, I cannot think of a single interview where the candidate was
   asked or expected to read a document. Nevertheless, they wear
   reading glasses and when spoken to tend to look over the top of
   them in order to clearly see who has asked the question. While it
   can give the impression of being an academic type, it can also
   project an attitude of aloofness and arrogance. Avoid this mannerism by not wearing reading glasses except when a document
   needs to be read during the interview.

8. *Staged characteristics.* I witnessed a large-city superintendent
   lose an opportunity to advance in a search because of her staged
   familiarity with the interviewers. Apparently, she had received
   coaching on her interviewing skills, and she was advised by her
   coach to use her new techniques during one of my searches. Unfortunately, what she engaged in was a regional, cultural practice
   that went over badly in a sophisticated, conservative Boston suburb. After the chairperson of the committee introduced her to
   the group as a whole (sixteen in number), the candidate decided
   to work her way around the table. This is not unusual in itself
   since many candidates want to shake hands with the committee
   members. But, in this case, she not only shook hands but also put

her arm around each committee member and chatted for a moment or two, all the while giving them a hug! It was a level of familiarity that she had not earned and a case of poor taste. It was also culturally inappropriate. As mentioned earlier, you must not embarrass interviewers.

9. *Attitude of superiority*. One candidate came to a search with outstanding credentials in terms of his successes, although he was not without controversy in his career. He was an intellectually powerful candidate but one who possessed a superior attitude that he brought into the interview room. There are few candidates who will turn off an interviewing committee faster than someone who gives the impression that he is a cut above them. His attitude was such that it signaled how fortunate the district would be if it hired him. Demonstrating a strong intellect is desirable, but the manner in which it is acted out is critical. Consider yourself one among equals. Avoid a bearing that diminishes interviewers.

10. *Repetitious behaviors*. One candidate had an odd way of acknowledging the interviewer whenever a question was asked. As soon as the question was completed, the candidate would look at the interviewer and give a little whistle. It was a little "whew"-type whistle, which inferred "That was some question! I'll see if I can handle it!" Just as in the case of the candidate with the mustache, where we all watched to see what he would do, likewise with this candidate as we waited on each whistle! If it were not such a childlike mannerism, it would have been humorous. Observing the interview, I couldn't help but wonder if, in unison, the interviewers were also going to whistle.

In the next chapter, "Out of the Gate," we discuss how to avoid early pitfalls in the interview.

⑫

OUT OF THE GATE

At this stage, you have done as much as possible to prepare yourself. In just a few minutes you will step into the room and be confronted with heavens knows what. What mood are the interviewers in? Has the chair adequately prepared them? Have they already seen a great candidate who is clearly the front-runner? Is someone waiting to confront you on the credibility of your resume and cover letter? Are you just so much ballast? Is the insider already appointed in the mind of the chair? Have the governing board or superintendent already expressed their reservations because of where you are from? Do you possess the educational pedigree desired? What role will affirmative action play in the selection? Are there racial, religious, or gender issues at play? You have no answers, only questions.

The best advice you can be given at this point is to ignore all of the above and assume the competition is wide open and that the interviewers will soon see in you the qualities they seek in the finalist for the position. Confidence in yourself is vital, especially since the lack of it will be apparent to most interviewers who are observing you.

DO IT RIGHT THE FIRST TIME

To some, the thought of an interview will be viewed as an accident waiting to happen; to others, it will be seen as an exhilarating experience and the ultimate job-hunt challenge. For you, it will be the latter because of the steps you have taken to get here, including the one that emphasized the necessity to be better prepared than all the other candidates. You did your homework. Now, you must pretend you are a stage actor, waiting for the curtain to rise before an audience that expects a spectacular performance. You have one opportunity. There are no retakes! An interview is a performance, a chance to demonstrate talent and a time to engage others in the event. It is what you have waited for. There is excitement about competing, and you need to project a sense of confidence upon entering the room. You must believe that, for perhaps the first time in your recruiting efforts, you finally know who you are, what you do best, what you can offer this district, and how to convince the interviewers of this. While other candidates will bring into the room their briefcases and documents that no one will be interested in, you will bring your wit and your confidence. Think "This job is mine."

As a consultant, I am sometimes concerned that the interviewers will not be as prepared as their candidates. It is disheartening to a candidate to prepare for an interview and then have it fall flat because of the lack of proficiency on the part of the interviewers. I worry that interviewers will be ignorant of good interviewing techniques or that the chair of the committee will not have structured the process, questions, scenario, and format to draw the best out of a candidate. I have been to such an interview, and there is little you can do except your best.

THE PROTOCOL OF THE INTRODUCTION

You are dressed appropriately, groomed discreetly, and enthusiastic about the interview when the chair of the committee comes to greet you. It is at this moment that the interview has been initiated, both for the chair and for you. When we are coaching the chair in our role as consultant, we make it clear that an interview can be damaged at the outset if the chair does not create a sincere, comfortable welcome. And so it is for the candidate. It is here that you will make a first impression on the chair, who usually has considerable influence on committee members. Look her in the eye, shake hands firmly, and introduce yourself with first and last name, but not your title. Let your resume speak to your credentials.

Hopefully, the chair will be experienced enough to engage in a bit of small talk to help settle you down, bring focus to the session, and share with you how the interview will be conducted. Usually, a chair will inform you that first names will be used and will ask by what name you would like to be addressed.

The chair will introduce you to the committee. "Ladies and gentlemen, allow me to introduce Abigail Anderson. She has traveled from Texas to be with us tonight. We welcome her to our community. Abigail has asked that you call her Abby." Then, to the candidate, "Abby, we'll go around the table and members of the committee will introduce themselves." At which point, introductions are usually by turn around the table. You have the option of either nodding acknowledgment when each name is mentioned or, if you prefer and if the room arrangements allow, you may move around the table and shake hands. There is no right or wrong way to introduce yourself to them but there are appropriate and inappropriate ways. Above all, be discreet. Earlier, I described a candidate who thought it appropriate to give each interviewer a hug and the negative impact it had on the interview. Depending upon what the committee has decided, members may or may not identify their positions although it is common practice for them to do so. Almost always, the members will want to be referred to by first names.

BE WATCHFUL OF THE TIME

As you respond to the introductions, it is vital that you take a count of the number of interviewers, each of whom expects that he will ask at least one question. Assume, for example, that there are nine members, a forty-five-minute interview, less the time needed for opening and closing statements of approximately two minutes each. This leaves a little more than four minutes on the average for you to answer a question. Deduct from that a couple of follow-up questions by the members, and you have three to three and a half minutes for each response. This is an average, and you will have to consider the importance of each question and apportion time accordingly. As simple as this suggestion seems, most candidates find it difficult to allot time efficiently. An assistant superintendent, seeking her first superintendent position, holds the record for the longest average answer, coming in at nine minutes per question. Presidential candidates only get two minutes!

Some chairs will be specific as to what the protocol will be in terms of how many questions will be asked, but most often the directions will be general. For that reason, you must assume that each interviewer will, at a minimum, be afforded the time to ask one question.

BE PREPARED FOR THE VERY FIRST QUESTION

Once you have taken your seat, the interview begins. Some committees like to begin with a content question, such as "What is your impression of our latest test scores in eighth-grade mathematics?" A content question has the advantage of letting you work in familiar territory at the outset. After all, the reason you are here is because you are a well-qualified professional who should know the answers to content questions. Given this opportunity, take advantage of it. It is the type of question I prefer that interviewing committees use. For the candidate, it is an opportunity to score points.

However, other committees prefer to give the candidate a warm-up question that may become the first unintentional booby trap for the candidate. The question usually goes something like this: "We have your resume and other application materials, but the members would appreciate you're taking a minute or two to touch upon the highlights of your career." If not that exact wording, it will be similar. In the hundreds of interviews I have monitored, it is this opening question relating to "highlights of your career" that worries me the most.

There is no way of knowing how the candidate will respond, but the one thing I am certain of is that most of the time the answer will be too long. I decided to clock many of the answers given by candidates to get a sense of the average time they consumed to respond to the opening question dealing with career highlights. The longest response time to an opening question on career highlights is approximately thirty minutes in the case mentioned earlier where a big-city superintendent used the time to display his charts and graphs. That was thirty minutes out of an hour interview. If I had not stopped him, he would have consumed the entire hour with his graphics.

The next-longest answer to the opening career highlights question was given by an experienced superintendent who used fourteen minutes out of a forty-five-minute interview to tip-toe across his career; what he really did was to stumble across his career. Although the chair of the interviewing committee has some responsibility to interrupt and get the candidate refocused on another question, the candidate has the primary responsibility to monitor his own response. The lesson here is to anticipate that this type of question will be asked since it is most frequently the one used to open an interview. Stand in front of a mirror with a stopwatch and sketch out a short response.

Know When to Stop Talking

I repeat a point made earlier, that the interviewers will often give the candidate a hint to stop. Some will say "Thank you" and hope you pick up the clue. Others will smile and nod as though to give finality to the answer. Some will fidget and some will twist and turn in their chairs. All of these are in addition to those who are looking at the ceiling. Then, of course, there are the doodlers who are such because they have lost interest. If a candidate is so insensitive as to not pick up on one or more of these hints, she does not deserve to be moved ahead in the process.

Reshaping the First Question to Your Advantage

We advise all candidates to consider the question, "Touch on the highlights of your career" as a way to make an "opening statement." The quality of this statement and a "closing statement" at the conclusion of the interview could be deciding factors for the interviewers in terms of moving you forward.

Consider the following response a superintendent candidate might use in response to the question posed about the "highlights of your career."

Thank you for the opportunity to meet with you today and share my background and experience with you. Since you have my application, cover letter, and resume, I would like to touch on the highlights of my career by reflecting for a minute or two on several of my mentors whose guidance and support were important factors in my establishing a successful career. Without their mentoring I would not be here today. They helped me create a work history that allows me to compete for this position of superintendent of schools in your district. All too often we believe that we alone shaped our careers when in fact so may others have played pivotal roles.

In my first position of assistant principal I learned from my principal that discipline was to be used to assist students and not to punish them. That mind-set allowed me to see students, not as kids in difficulty and who had to be turned around, but as young adults who needed still another guiding hand. In my first principal position, I learned from the members of my faculty that there were many hands to help me when the going got tough and the only price I was expected to pay for that help was to remember that teachers and support staff were colleagues whose voices needed to be heard and whose advice was valuable.

And now, as assistant superintendent, I work for a superintendent whose every action demonstrates that respect for one another will ultimately bring success to all of our joint endeavors. I have been fortunate to have had teachers, administrators, and support staff as my moral and ethical mentors. Many lessons have been learned, and if I am chosen to lead this district, I would commit myself to bringing those same values to this position. I would want to be thought of as a mentor of others. The highlights of my career are the times I spent with outstanding mentors.

The opening statement can be expanded upon and must be tailored to fit the situation. The statement above is not meant to be the only way to open an interview; it is simply one way. There are many other messages you can deliver while answering the question. It is a better approach than boring interviewers with details they already possess. It is important that you begin to move out ahead of the competition at the very outset of the interview.

If the first question asked of you is a content-based one, the risk of making an error is slim. There have been very few questions asked in the hundreds of interviews I have monitored that caught a candidate without a reasonable response. The two exceptions deal with local test scores and local demographics. There are candidates who fail to anticipate these questions. It is especially true of candidates from out of state. Local test scores should always be analyzed, and every candidate should have good data pertaining to racial, ethnic, economic, and gender makeup of the district, including the student population, resident population, and the composition of the certified and classified staffs.

When the Correct Answer Really Counts

A second question often asked to begin an interview session is "Why do you want this job?" If there was ever an opportunity to hit a home run, this is it. Yet I'm reminded of three instances when the answer to this question essentially stopped an interview in its tracks. The interview went on but the candidate was, for all practical purposes, out of the running. One candidate responded with "I need the insurance." I recall a second candidate stating "The job is close to home." And a third who noted that "he would be able to double dip" since he could take retirement in another state! How indiscreet can you be? Needless to say, all were terrible responses and did not help the candidates. While all three answers are legitimate in the minds of the candidates, there was no reason why they would share them with an interviewing committee.

The answer to the question "Why do you want this job" will vary with each candidate. For one candidate it may be a logical career move, while for another it may be the challenge of leading an underperforming district. For others it may the opportunity to join a district where a new leadership team is being assembled. Or perhaps it is being able to work with an alternative school. Whatever the case, you must be able to articulate a legitimate reason why you would make a professional move. Interviewers will see through insincere answers designed to impress them. Stumbling on this essential question will stall your interview.

SLOW STARTERS ARE USUALLY SLOW FINISHERS

I have listened to candidates in private job-coaching sessions relate to me that they are slow starters in interviews and that they gain momentum as the interview progresses. I ask them to visualize a horse race where the thoroughbreds are being pushed and cajoled into the starting gates, nervous and anxious, difficult to steady, some terrified, others spirited, but all waiting for the gate to open. When that gate does open, no horse can afford to stumble. Each must quickly break out of the pack before being injured or pushed aside. As a candidate, you cannot afford to have a slow start because you lose your opportunity to get to the rail. You must not stumble, because the others will open distance on you. When the interview opens, you must get out in front and never give up the lead. You head for the rail and stay there. Failure belongs to others, not to you. If you are not a thoroughbred in your profession, you should not be on this interviewing track—and it is this track that we turn to in the next chapter.

13

ON TO THE TRACK

You left the gate with your opening statement. Hopefully you did not stumble, or if you did, not so badly that you cannot remain competitive on the interviewing track. Regardless of how well you did on the first question, the interview is underway and the interviewers begin to take measure of you as the candidate. This measurement is taken not just by the words expressed but also by other factors such as mannerisms, poise, and level of confidence, to mention just a few. It is now that you want to avoid any serious interviewing errors. Stumbling on the opening question, while not a good start, is not fatal. The real test now begins. The mantra at this stage of the search process is "distance, distance, and distance!" Move away from the pack but remain close to the interviewing committee.

Occasionally an experienced jockey will make a mistake or will be riding a mount that just does not have it that day. But, on the whole, once out of the gate, inexperienced jockeys who have never been in a high-stakes race will make the most mistakes. This analogy is appropriate for the competitive interviewing you are about to experience. Experienced administrators tend to make mistakes because they let their pride get in the way of effective training. However, most often it will be the inexperienced administrator who will get into serious trouble. Nevertheless, we are all prone to stumbling unless we have prepared for the interview.

THIRTY-FOUR INTERVIEWING ERRORS

The following thirty-four serious interviewing errors were observed and documented during actual interviews. They are not in order of importance; rather, they are in the order that I recorded them over many interview sessions. They are not the only errors recorded but they are serious enough that you should avoid making them. As noted throughout this book, every error or mistake described is attached to a candidate with whom I have worked and who was competing for a position. Some of these candidates, once they made errors and were willing to take advice, went on to other successful interviews. Others chose not to seek assistance and floundered in their quest for a new position. Experienced and inexperienced candidates alike failed to heed the truth of "Pride goeth before the fall."

If you have been recruiting and have failed to progress beyond the first or second interview, it may be because you committed one or more of these errors. As you review each one, you need to ask yourself "Does this describe me?"

1. If you want to think about a response to a question asked, do not look at the ceiling, desk, or walls for inspiration unless you believe someone wrote the answers on one of those surfaces. The best strategy is to look directly at the person who asked the question, take a couple of seconds to collect your thoughts, and then respond. Earlier I described an assistant superintendent who was appointed superintendent against heavy odds. It was a male-dominated board, and the other six finalists were all male. At the outset, the chair stated that she was in last place in his mind. She eventually won all members over because of the thoughtful manner in which she responded and the depth of her answers. They saw a candidate who thought before she spoke, a quality many administrators have not mastered.

2. There are several methods one can use in responding to a question. Many candidates make the mistake of beginning to answer a question before the interviewer has completed the question. In this situation, the candidate is initiating a response without fully understanding what is being asked. Impetuousness is not a qual-

ity that a board or superintendent seeks in a candidate. Another method of responding is for the candidate to begin nodding his head before the question is completed, once again signaling that he knows what is coming. Unless clairvoyance is in his repertoire, there is no way to fully understand what is about to be asked. This sends a message that the candidate is not an effective listener. Unlike impetuous behavior that is to be shunned, listening is a quality that is sought. A third method of responding is to look everywhere except at the interviewer. Interpersonal skills rank at the top of the list of qualities associated with the most successful administrators. When a candidate avoids eye contact with others, it sends a powerful message that she lacks the personal touch so important in a service business.

3. How then does a candidate respond to a question, the answer to which needs to be thoughtfully framed? I refer to the candidate noted earlier who overcame board bias and then moved into the winner's circle based in large measure on her interviewing skills, both with the interviewing committee and with a larger public audience later in the process. In her case, she listened carefully to the entire question before answering, she did not start moving her head up and down and all around as though she could not wait to respond to a question that had yet to be completed, and she did not look at the table, ceiling, or walls. Instead, she looked directly into the eyes of the questioner, paused while she collected her thoughts, and responded. Then, while answering the question, she made eye contact with everyone at the table. Today, I use her as the best case of effective interviewing. However, as effective an interviewer as she was, she also brought to the table solid experience and a thorough understanding of the superintendent's role.

A second assistant superintendent with whom we worked, and who was painfully shy, would always look down at the table or off to the side. Her failure to look at the interviewer for any length of time was distracting to the committee and sent a powerful negative message. The impression she was creating was one of very poor interpersonal skills. After sharing with her the techniques described above and used by a successful candidate, she greatly improved her interviewing techniques. While she will perhaps never be as adept at interviewing as the first candidate mentioned, she gained sufficient confidence to compete successfully and reach the winner's circle as superintendent. Nevertheless, during her last appearance in a successful superintendent search, she "wowed" the public audience with what can only be described as a charming, personal, and warm question-and-answer session. She displayed a sense of confidence.

4. As long as we are speaking about the ceiling, you must read the interviewers because if they are looking at the ceiling, you really are in trouble! While you must answer the question, you also need to understand that there is only so much they want to hear. Their looking at the ceiling usually indicates that your answer is either too long or is irrelevant. When coaching, we stress that you need to answer the question asked and not the one you hoped would be asked. The most dramatic case of a candidate answering a question that had not been asked relates to an assistant superintendent from a large urban district as he competed for a superintendent position in an average-sized community. As part of his graduate school program, he had prepared an "entry plan" that his advisor had emphasized as being vital to any new job. I agree that at some point in the process you may have to articulate how you would make your entry—but you need to pick the right time. This candidate chose the wrong time. He was determined, at this first screening interview, to let the interviewers know he had an entry plan and was determined to explain it in detail, in spite of the fact that no one asked about it, and as it turned out, no one was interested. He waited for what he thought was an opening in the discussion and then made his thrust! It was painful to watch the interviewers. All were annoyed that he entered into the discussion a topic that none of them considered relevant at this stage. To get him back on track, one of the interviewers mercifully tossed him a softball question that he proceeded to drop. I paraphrase the soft question: "We are short of instructional space in the district at all secondary grade levels. We are also short on time to create space. How would you address this issue?"

For an assistant superintendent in a large district, he should have hit this out of the park. But his response was, and again I paraphrase, "I'd look in the community for available rooms." How shallow an answer when you consider the many other options he could have offered, such as revamping the schedule, new programming, split sessions, block scheduling, extended year, use of vacation time, and temporary classrooms, among others. He lost an opportunity to demonstrate both creativity and good problem-solving skills when he introduced a topic that was not relevant. No sooner was this candidate out of the gate and on to the track but that he stumbled badly. The lesson is, don't answer a question that wasn't asked.

5. Undoubtedly, somewhere along the recruiting trail, you will be asked to discuss student grouping practices. It is one of the handfuls of questions that seem to be of interest in all districts. The question will be framed something like, "How effective is heterogeneous grouping in the primary grades?" Whatever you do, do not fall into the trap of responding with "There's a lot of research out there" unless you can cite specific research by a credible researcher. Otherwise, someone on the committee will ask you to be specific. If you are unable to provide data, you will have lost this point. Whether the question is about student grouping practices, social promotion, or any other controversial topic, stay clear of the comment "There is research out there" unless you are prepared to provide the data and their sources.

6. Invariably, you will be asked what you have recently read and to give your impression of it—that is, a short book report! Thus, you should have read something you can speak to with accuracy, authority, and clarity. The worst sin you can commit on this question is to indicate you have read a certain book when in fact you have not. It was mentioned earlier that a very strong candidate lied about a book he said he read and when questioned by an interviewer was unable to provide any detail. Over the years, I have been surprised at how many candidates have been unable to name one or two books that they have read recently.

7. Another favorite question is "Name your heroes" and why. It is not a question I am particularly fond of but I alert candidates to

the fact that it will often be raised. When a candidate is stumped, she will mention a parent, a former supervisor, and one or two national figures, among whom most often mentioned are Martin Luther King and John F. Kennedy. Anticipating that it may be asked, you would do well to think about the question ahead of time. As irrelevant as the question is, you score significant points if you articulate why the person you named is a hero. It is also helpful if you can define hero.

8. It is quite common to be asked what role athletics and extracurricular activities play in the education of students. Most candidates will handle this with a sense of balance, but a good number tend to dwell on the importance of athletics to the extent that they sound as though they are competing for the position of athletic director. If the district's governing board wanted an AD for a superintendent, it would have advertised the position as such. The lesson to be learned is that athletics serve one constituency, but there are large numbers of students to whom other extracurricular activities are equally important. As an administrator, you represent all students and therefore must provide for all of them in your responses.

9. Candidates who were raised in households where it is common practice to use hands to make a point while talking need to take special care during an interview. One of my strongest superintendent candidates possessed a pathological need to point her finger at the interviewers to make a point when responding. The fact is, she was and remains a very dominant educator, but that is not her defining quality once you know her. However, that dominant mannerism cost her a job her first time out. With forthright advice, she kept this mannerism under control. She learned her lesson well and went on to a successful interview and an appointment to a superintendent position. I worked with another candidate who was in a superintendent position and desired to move to another state for reasons of pension benefits. Between the first and second time I met with her for initial discussions about her potential move, she had taken coaching lessons from someone who emphasized the use of gesturing and hand movements as a way to keep the attention of the interviewers and to emphasize

certain points. I thought for a few minutes that I was observing a robot. This was no longer the same person I worked with previously. The movements were orchestrated, artificial, and annoying. I suggested that she put an end to the movements and return to her more natural style.

10. Being sensitive to time during the interview is to your advantage. There will be questions that do not require an extensive response, so do not waste time on them. Others will need comprehensive coverage to make your points. Time management is important in any position you hold, and this interview is the time to practice it. You need to know when you have answered the question. When you have done so, stop! The reason answers tend to run too long is because candidates want to provide far too much detail. They believe they have shortchanged the interviewers if they do not address every nuance. All of us have worked with or for colleagues who simply ran one sentence into another, never coming up for breath. They never knew when to stop and never learned how to listen. You must not fall into that trap. Often, an interviewer will give you a clue when he is satisfied that you have given sufficient data by simply saying, "Thank you." If you get such a clue, stop! You should be thankful a clue was given because being long winded is among the most common of interviewing errors. What may happen is that the interviewers, some of whom will be your employees, are asking themselves, "Do I really want to work with this nonstop talker day in and day out?"

11. To exaggerate is to run the risk of becoming unbelievable. For example, I recall the following question being asked, "Superintendents usually have multiple issues to cope with each day. How would you prioritize your work so that everything gets done when it needs to get done?" The response was, "That's not a problem. I make hundreds of decisions every day. I am used to decision making. I am able to address all issues." Few who were present at the interview believed that response. As a former experienced superintendent, I didn't believe it. A better response might have been, "One of the skills superintendents develop over time is the ability to sort through many issues and settle on those that need attention immediately versus those that can be deferred. Rushing to conclusions

on many issues is a blueprint for trouble. In general, I deal first with those that are health and safety related, followed by returning calls that have an imperative message, and then meeting with others who have urgent issues to be tended to. Involving others in the decision-making process allows both me and the district to deal effectively with many matters simultaneously."

12. Language usage continues to be a problem for many candidates. Some poor language usage is committed out of ignorance, which does not speak well for the training of some educators, and at other times it is a misreading of the audience, believing that colloquial speech is appropriate. Interviewers do not want to hear any off-color words, comments, or jokes. No matter how appropriate you may think such words or comments are, you are bound to offend some at the table. An outstanding candidate for a regional school district superintendent position used the word "crap" in response to a question. No matter what the question was, the word is inappropriate under all circumstances. From that moment on, he was in the interview but out of contention. Another candidate in different search used the word "dimwit." He did so at a public session. While it was clear to me that he did not use it in a derogatory way or to classify students, it is a word that has disappeared from our vocabulary in this age of special-needs students. There was a cacophony of protest from the audience, and it was picked up by the local paper and reported in a negative manner. Another used the word *stupid* in reference to himself, which probably was an apt description.

13. Avoid "war stories" whenever possible. There is a tendency to answer questions by relating to past experiences. "When I was in Peoria" stories are common. Unless you are asked to give an illustration from your past as to how you addressed an issue, you are best advised to answer the question in terms of how you would approach it in the new district, given its unique set of circumstances. What works in your current district may not work in this district. This is one strong reason why you need to investigate the district you are applying to so as to have good background data. Your professional history is important as a prediction of success but it is not a blueprint for future action.

14. Occasionally, I monitor an interview in which the candidate is intent upon dropping important names from the lexicon of American educators. If you want to annoy the working members of the interview committee, this is as good a way as any. Most of them have been hunkered down with their daily routines and rarely get out to high-powered meetings or conventions. Many are not in education and therefore the names mean little or nothing to them. The last thing they want to hear about is your hobnobbing with great American educators.

15. Unless there is a specific purpose to be served, I suggest you refrain from quoting great poets and scholars. While quoting great scholars may serve on occasion to enhance a response, it more often than not comes across as rehearsed. When someone uses poetry to make a point, it most often comes across as contrived. Much like the candidate who could not wait to describe his "entry plan," the poet candidate is also waiting for an opening to display the classical nature of his education. Any hint of insincerity by the candidate will leave a negative impression with interviewers.

16. Failing to tell the truth can set you up for an embarrassing interview. I once worked with a candidate for whom I had the greatest respect in terms of her integrity. She was asked a question relating to whether she received professional help for a personally trait that impacted her work. The interviewer asking the question already knew the answer! It was not an illegal question to ask, but a thoughtless one that should not have been asked. Had I known in advance that it was to be asked, I would not have permitted it because it was negative in intent. Like the candidate, I was caught off guard. The candidate answered in the negative and, of course, her not being totally truthful ended this job search for her. This was a situation wherein there was no satisfactory answer. In retrospect, the best response would have been to politely refuse to answer since it trespassed into a personal area that was out of bounds. A non-response would not have been any worse than not telling the truth. Telling the truth may also have also ended her chances, but there was always the probability that some of the interviewers would have been impressed with her forthrightness. The lesson to be learned is that if there is something in your background that

could be damaging, chances are that someone else knows about it. Be prepared to deal with it when and if it comes up or do not apply for the position if you can reasonably assume that the disclosure of it will end your candidacy.

17. While I strongly urge candidates not to tell jokes, laughing at yourself and introducing humor are good vehicles that help demonstrate your lightheartedness. This is not a life-or-death situation. Most interviewers want to know that in addition to your serious professional nature, you also have a lighter side. Most interviews provide ample opportunity and raw material to use as sources of humor. However, in my experience, most attempts at telling jokes have fallen flat. It is best not to plan to interject humor artificially; rather, wait for a natural opening in the conversation to laugh at yourself.

18. There are two words that I strongly advise experienced and older candidates never to mention: retirement and pension. You will be considered a short-timer with many interviewers if you suggest that you are "close to retirement" and that this would be a great way to "close out your career." If you use the word "retirement," the chances are you just closed out a career in this district. The word "retirement" used in any context simply sends the wrong message. The second word is the most dangerous of all: "pension." The mere mention of the word sends up warning flares, including the image that you must be "old" if you have qualified for a pension. This is a case where perception is reality in the eyes of the interviewers. Keep in mind that age discrimination is illegal and questions that address age in any context cannot be entered into the conversation by the interviewers, so why would you do so? Once you provide an opening, you afford interviewers an opportunity to pursue the subject. On the bright side, there are districts that recruit candidates who are close to retirement or who have retired in another state. I have done so on behalf of clients. It is done primarily because the hiring district has a wage scale that is not competitive. By employing someone from another state who can take early retirement or who is retired, the new district can pay a lower rate since it is a second income to the candidate.

19. In response to the question "Why are you interested in this position?" it is not uncommon for the candidate to respond with, "This is a great district with an outstanding cadre of administrators. To work with them would be the highlight of my career" or something similar. It sounds good, but this is very dangerous road for you to travel. First, you probably have no basis for knowing if the board considers its administrative staff outstanding. Whatever feedback you have about the administrative staff has usually come from one of the administrators in the district. Why would any administrator consider colleagues anything but outstanding? But, from the board's perspective, it may have little positive to say about its administrative staff and may be seeking a new superintendent to clean house! If you are applying for a building-level administrative position, you, too, need to be careful about commenting on the outstanding quality of any person in the district since the superintendent about to employ you may want you to engage in some house cleaning. The lesson is to simply avoid offering any opinion about the quality of the present staff.

20. Making a comment about the quality of the administrative or teaching staff without good data says something negative about your investigative skills. If you want to be a sleuth, be a good one. Unless you have a solid basis to assess the staff, stay away from the issue. I have been in attendance at many interviews when superintendent candidates in particular have referred to an outstanding team when in fact the board was looking to get rid of some key members of the "outstanding" team and was assessing the candidate from that perspective. Invariably, board members in this situation are asking themselves, "Is this candidate tough enough to take on and get rid of two principals, the business manager, and the director of personnel?" Unfortunately, board members are not always forthcoming with the candidate as to how they view the administrative staff. Before you answer the question "Why do you want this position?" think carefully before you mention the quality of the staff.

21. How often have you said in response to a question from one of the interviewers, "That's a great question!" Occasionally, the

question is a great one. Most often it is simply a question that had not been posed to you before. If the last question was a great one, how about all of the other questions from the other interviewers who are present? Were their questions not great? Were they not worthy of comment? Your job is not to evaluate the questions, but simply to answer them. You need to keep all of the interviewers on your team. Interviewers are real people and are as sensitive about being slighted as you are. The best approach is to accept the question for what it is and answer it as effectively and directly as you can.

22. Some readers may be old enough to remember the Perry Mason mystery series, which still appears on TV reruns today. For those who are not old enough, Perry Mason was a genius of a trial lawyer who always outwitted the district attorney who disliked Perry and went out of his way to raise questions that he hoped would trip up Perry. Perry's famous stalling tactic, when he was not prepared to give an immediate answer to the district attorney, was to light up a cigarette and take a few puffs. Those few seconds provided valuable time for him to frame a response. I do not suggest you light up a cigarette, but there are moments when you need thinking time. The best device was described earlier, and that is to simply look the interviewer in the eye and hesitate for a moment or two before answering. Interviewers appreciate your thoughtfulness. Another device is to say something, such as "Let me see if I fully understand what you are asking," and then repeat the question to gain some time. Used too often, it will be viewed as a negative tactic. Used with discretion, it is an effective way to gain time to think. I believe that those familiar with education place a premium on candidates who are not impulsive in answering questions. Teachers, in particular, are very much aware of how different students require varying response times and therefore individualize instruction so that students who are not the first to raise their hands are still provided an opportunity to be heard. Adults also differ in the amount of time they need to frame responses. It is perfectly acceptable to take your time.

23. In response to a potentially controversial question, the answer to which you are undecided, you do not want to respond with some-

thing like, "I'm flexible on that." On the other hand, you also want to avoid taking such a hard stand that you are unable to retreat from it as the search process goes on. I am thinking of a strong candidate who took a philosophical position on advanced placement that almost knocked him out of the running. His position was that advanced placement courses should only be provided for the strongest students and that placements should be by prerequisites. This interview occurred at a time when all advanced placement barriers were being lifted in this district and all students were encouraged to take these courses without meeting any prerequisites. Had he taken a position wherein he generally supported advanced placement for all students and indicated that he had certain reservations, he would have had an easier time to restate his case. As it happened, the rest of his interview was superb and he was invited back based on the strength of the interview. At the second interview, without prompting, he asked if he could restate his position on advanced placement courses. He did and it was well received. Did he back off his position? No, he did not, but if appointed to the position, he said he would commit himself to implementing and maintaining the policy position of the board. You may ask how can you believe one thing and promote another? The fact is, all superintendents implement some board policies to which they do not personally ascribe. Many building principals support directives from their superintendents with which they disagree. Teachers follow orders from principals that they would prefer to ignore. The rule of thumb in these situations is that if what you are being asked to support is not illegal or morally or ethically in conflict with your own beliefs and standards of conduct, then you can justify implementing the policies of others.

24. Most candidates are proud of their children and take every opportunity to brag somewhat about them. However, where you do this bragging is important. Candidates should shy away from bringing their family affairs into an interview in any way unless asked to do so. Take the example of the advanced placement matter mentioned earlier. It would be easy to slip into a situation where you might say, "My daughter took several advanced placement courses and they

were invaluable when she entered Stanford." Who really cares about the personal experience of your daughter? I have listened as candidates stated that their children graduated from prestigious colleges or universities. Believe me, it is of no interest to interviewers. Where you went to college may be of some interest, but where your children went to school is irrelevant. The danger is that the children of the interviewers may have attended "no name" schools, or may not have attended college at all. Interviewers do not need to be reminded of how their children compare with yours.

25. Candidates need to remember that while only one interviewer at a time will ask the question, all of the others will generally be interested in the answer. It is critically important that after you have begun your response by looking first at the questioner, you must make eye contact with everyone else at the table on every question if at all possible. If you concentrate only on the questioner, you will not be able to assess what impact your response is having on the other members. All interviewers want to be engaged all of the time. It is to your advantage to keep all of them focused on you. The most dramatic case I have had regarding lack of eye contact was with a principal who was competing for a superintendent position. I thought highly enough of his credentials to include him in the search. After he completed his interview and left the room, almost with one voice, the female interviewers said that not once did he make eye contact with any of them. He was very quickly labeled a chauvinist and eliminated. I have no idea if this was true or not, but it did not matter because a good number of the interviewers thought he was, and they did not want him as their next superintendent.

26. Once a comment is out of your mouth, there is no taking back the words. Therefore, think for a moment about stage actors who perform before live audiences as compared to movie or TV performers who can redo scenes. At an interview you are a stage actor engaged in a live performance with one opportunity to say what you need to say and to leave a positive impression. There are no retakes. So, one lesson to be learned is to think before you speak. And when you are ready to do so, think like a stage actor and reflect upon how his perfect diction, voice modulation, good eye

contact, appropriate gesturing, and body language create images. Often, it is what they do not say that sends powerful messages. Outstanding actors are fabulous at sending nonverbal messages to the audience. Let no one dissuade you from the fact that interviewing is part theater. While it is inappropriate for you to "play a role" that is not you, it is quite appropriate to use the subtleties of the stage actor to impress interviewers.

27. Interviewers want to know how inclusive you are as a leader. If you have a record of being a collaborative type, it will almost naturally show during your interview. Nevertheless, you must use "we" more often that you use "I." I can think of no school leader who became outstanding by going it alone. Without the efforts of a competent staff, most leaders would be average leaders. Many of the interviewers could end up being your colleagues if you get this position. This is a chance for you to show them who you really are and how you relate to others. If they have been properly trained as interviewers, they know that "what they see is what they get." Make certain they see the real and capable you.

28. When asked to give an example, give one, not several. There is a tendency for candidates to answer the question asked and then, not having confidence in what it is they said, repeat the answer with different words. If the interviewers did not understand the answer or thought it incomplete, one or more will ask for an expansion. Do not use your valuable minutes traveling in reverse!

29. Avoid name-dropping, such as "I know a bit about this town because my brother-in-law is the first selectman." If having a brother-in-law as first selectman is important, and if he is influential, you can rest assured he would already have made it known. However, anytime you infuse the name of a prominent local figure, politician or otherwise, into the interview process you may have started down a slippery slope. Interviewers do not want to believe that their decisions will be overridden by politics.

30. Do not take credit for the work of others. It is fascinating to observe candidates, especially those high up in the administrative hierarchy, lay claim to significant improvements in their current district in spite of the fact they may have been there only a year or two. They fail to acknowledge the work of their predecessors.

It leaves the impression that the district was an academic desert until they arrived. And once there, they sprinkled magic powder and all the teachers and administrators suddenly awakened. My most recent relevant case occurred when an assistant superintendent in a large district stated to me that in less than ten months he turned the secondary schools around, something that escaped many talented senior administrators before him! As it happened, he left the district shortly thereafter to take a building-level position.

31. Do not address any one interviewer by first name unless you refer to all of them by first names. Inside candidates are more apt to fall prey to this, although occasionally there will be an outside candidate who knows one or more of the interviewers. Creating an even playing field is as much the candidate's responsibility as it is that of the interviewing committee interviewers.

32. Do not use the interview to lecture the committee members. You should know more about any subject raised in an interview than any of the others present. Presumably, that is the reason they consider you worthy to be part of this discussion. However, in presenting your knowledge, refrain from lecturing the interviewers— otherwise they may view you as talking down to them.

33. Interviewers will invariably ask how you process parent complaints. Regardless of where you are on the chart of organization or what your title may be, you need to be careful in answering this question. The fact is that if you want to be hurled out of the running immediately, simply answer as follows: "In my district problems are solved at lowest level. A parent is expected to talk first with the teacher, and if that doesn't work out, then move on to the assistant principal, followed by the principal, then the deputy superintendent, and so forth." With that response, the interviewers, many of whom have children of their own, are now thinking that it might take a parent until the end of the academic term to actually get to talk to the superintendent! A humanist, and that is what you are as an administrator, understands that there are times when it is imperative for parents or students to start at the top. Avoid a hard and fast hierarchical approach to student and parent problems. Such an approach is simplistic and fails to consider the many

reasons why it is best to start at positions other than at the bottom. Think of yourself as the "sweeper" in a curling event. Your job is to sweep the ice clean just ahead of the curling stone so it can slide unimpeded and smoothly. Clearing the way for parents is the responsibility of the leader. Your task is to sweep away impediments.

34. Finally, keep family out of the interview. When I first thought about becoming involved in consultant work, I attended a number of sessions put on by national consultants to assess how they worked. At one session in particular, the consultant shared with the audience that every year he took his family to the top of Pike's Peak to meditate on the year ahead and to establish the goals that the family would use as a guide for the year ahead. Then he shared with us a notebook in which he kept a chronological, pictorial history of his family beginning with his marriage and up to the very day of the presentation at which I was present. And, page by page, he went through the notebook, explaining every event and detailing every photograph. I can't remember seeing an audience turned off so completely. Just prior to the time this guide went to press, I was conducting a search and one of three finalists was presenting before a governing board. Without warning, the candidate unzipped a briefcase and took out a very large notebook similar to the one described above. With agonizing deliberation, he marched all of us through marriage, career, births, and schooling for self, spouse, and children, all supported by pictures. It was an Ozzie and Harriet scene. My reaction this time was identical to when I experienced it so many years ago while attending the seminar of a national consultant. It is in poor taste to introduce your family and its history into an interview. You must avoid it at all costs. A professional portfolio, if requested, is one thing, but a personal trip through memory lane is gauche.

Now we move on to "Heading Home" and your closing statements to the interviewing committee.

14

HEADING HOME:
CLOSING STATEMENTS

Chapter 12, "Out of the Gate," referred to the importance of an opening statement and how to use it to kick-start an interview. It is a powerful tool if properly executed. In chapter 13, you reviewed thirty-four interviewing errors, and now you are "Heading Home" with a closing statement. The closing statement can serve one of three purposes:

First, in the event you were not completely satisfied with your overall presentation to the interviewing committee, the closing statement could be an opportunity for you to take the initiative to fill in the blanks. However, this is easier said than done. Attempting to reconstruct answers to multiple questions that were asked is usually not feasible and in most cases will be ineffective. But I have observed candidates attempting it.

Second, the closing statement can be employed to expand upon responses you made that could use further explanation. The most vivid recollection I have of a candidate attempting this was in relation to a prior question asked of him that dealt with technology. To begin with, let me say that I have rarely heard a candidate, whether an entry-level administrator or a senior administrator, deal effectively with a technology question. The following is an example of a technology question, typical of those often asked, along with a typical response. "Tell us what you are presently doing in the field of technology in your district?" Most likely what you will hear in return from the candidate is an inventory of what hardware and software is available to kids, future purchasing plans, a few words about Internet access, and some thoughts on training. There will be no depth to the answer because the question is so simplistic and the required answer so complex.

On the other hand, a question of substance to be considered by the interviewers might be stated as follows: "In describing technology in schools, educators usually refer to hardware and software acquisitions as though these are the essential underpinnings of the plan. While they are important, the committee would like to hear what your ideal technology plan is in conceptual terms, what is realistically within the grasp of public school systems with limited or decreasing financial resources, and the foundation of which is not the purchase of still more hardware and software. We are interested in specific learning outcomes and what purpose they serve."

A candidate was given this question during the course of his interview. His response was wretched. The interviewers were glassy eyed. Finally, all stumbled on to the next question. Then, when given a chance to give a closing statement, he decided to shift into reverse and attack the technology question once again. He would have been better advised to go fast forward and get out of there. His second attempt was an utter failure. His returning to this question was like trying to glue together the pieces of a crystal glass dropped on the floor. Best to just sweep it up. Do not try to repair that which is impossible to repair!

Remember that the purpose of this guide is to assist you in making a strong first impression and presentation, to create a powerful opening statement, and to engage in a strong and effective question-and-answer session. If all has gone well to this point, then the closing statement serves a purpose entirely different from the two reasons just mentioned.

The third and valid purpose of a closing statement is to end the interview running full tilt for the finish line. Just as you gave thought to how you would construct an opening statement, you need to do the same for the closing statement. For the final two or three minutes of the interview, you can be on center stage. Assume for a moment that your performance so far has been well received. The final minutes are when the strong climax should occur. Think theater, wherein the audience knows that this is the final scene of the final act; there is an air of anticipation. They expect to leave the theater fulfilled. This is your final moment to leave the interviewers with a positive attitude about you. The other candidates have come and gone. Most will not have had an outstanding opening statement, some will have had a quality interview, but few will have given thought to a powerful closing statement. The opportunity is yours to seize. Actors live for the moment when they can have center stage, alone, to "bring down the house." The stage is yours.

ASK NO QUESTIONS

Let us examine how events are likely to unfold. The question-and-answer session is over. If the consultant properly advised the chair, the latter will take the initiative in asking if you would like to make concluding remarks. If so, then the stage is yours.

However, the more likely scenario is that the chair will not offer an opportunity to make a closing statement. Rather, he is more apt to ask if you have any questions for the committee. If this occurs, then you have a chance to take control of the last two or three minutes of the interview.

Unless this is a final or semifinal stage interview where you might be negotiating a contract, you should not have any questions. None at all! I cannot think of a single question that is so important as to consume two or three of the most valuable minutes you may ever have to compete for this position. Only a fool would waste this moment!

The answers to any routine questions you may have regarding what happens next, when will you hear of the committee decision, what is the schedule, how many candidates are there, and so on are of no value because what will be will be. Your knowing the answers serves no useful purpose. Therefore, do not ask any questions.

THIS IS NO TIME FOR PHILOSOPHY

As for philosophical questions you may wish to pose, keep in mind that there is no one person on the committee who can answer questions of a philosophical nature for the entire committee. For example, who on the committee is qualified to answer the question, "What major challenges will the superintendent face in the next twelve months?" Obviously, no one knows the answer although each may think he or she does. Only the governing board can respond to the question. The point is that any answer from the interviewers is not only worthless, but also costly to you in terms of time lost. Therefore, do not waste valuable moments seeking irrelevant information. You should also avoid asking for information that is readily available to you from the office staff.

TAKE THE INITIATIVE WITH A CLOSING STATEMENT

If you are asked the question, "Do you have any questions of the committee?" pounce on this offer and use the time to make a closing statement. This is one example of how you can take the initiative.

> Thank you, madam chairman (or a less formal title depending upon how the interview was structured), for the opportunity to raise questions. However, as a result of the many wide-ranging questions raised by the committee, I have learned a great deal about the district and what it seeks in your new administrator (or the specific position for which you are competing). If I am fortunate enough to be asked to continue in the process, there will be questions I need to ask. But at this stage I have sufficient information. With your permission, I would like to leave you with a few final thoughts about my candidacy.

It is at this time that you deliver your final thoughts.

Once you have forged ahead politely, it is time to leave the committee with strong positive thoughts about you. Since you now have a better sense of what they are looking for through the questions asked, the materials published, and official information you received from the district, you are able to respond accordingly. If you were an outstanding listener during the interview, you also have formed a perception as to the profile of the person being sought and the issues that face the district. Keep in mind that you do not want to pretend you are someone other than who you are. You do not want to let them believe you can solve all the problems of the district. You don't need this job so badly as to project a false self. On the other hand, if you are an exceptional candidate with a broad range of experiences and a track record of continued successes, there is little you cannot deal with in this position. You may conclude that this is a position in which you can be successful. Therefore, you now need to convince the interviewers. Up to this point in the process, you have done well. Before the curtain drops on this final scene, you need to bring the interview to an exciting conclusion. You want an encore! Figuratively, you want them on their feet.

YOUR AUDIENCE AWAITS

If there was even a moment in time when speaking extemporaneously is valuable, it is now. You will have only a few seconds to formulate thoughts that address the district's needs as interpreted through the questions and the body language of interviewers as they reacted to your answers. Additionally, you need to speak from the heart about who you are and what you stand for. This is a stage, you are the star, and the audience of interviewers wants desperately to identify an outstanding finalist. You can make it happen.

The following is but one idea. It is for you to tailor your comments to the exact conditions at the time.

> I applied for this position in the belief that I could address the issues of the district as they had been outlined and that I could present a leadership profile that reflects what has been described in your literature. But, as often happens, the reality of a situation doesn't always parallel what has been advertised. As a result, a candidate has to be prepared to deal with this discrepancy. I was prepared to do just that, but as this interview has progressed and as I have listened to the questions raised, it appears to me that as a group you reflect the ideals of the district and represent a larger constituency. I like what has been implied in your questions and in your responses to my answers. There is little question in my mind that in applying for this position I made the correct decision. If the questions you raised reflect what is of concern and what needs to be addressed, then this is the right district for me at this time in my career. If the qualities you seek are those that you have referenced throughout this interview, then I believe that I am the appropriate person for this position. If you, as interviewers, are somewhat of a mirror image of the larger community, then

the workplace would be a comfortable one in which to work. All of this is a way of saying that I would be honored to be your next (fill in the blank). I thank each of you for the opportunity to meet today and to present my credentials. I hope you will conclude that I am the person you seek.

Once the chair has concluded the interview, you need to assess whether or not it is appropriate to shake hands with each member. If not, then you simply extend thanks and leave.

Now it is time to examine the makeup of interviewing committees and the motives of the participants.

15

PLEASE, WHO'S ASKING?

You are in the interview, the first question is raised, and you would really like to say, "Who's asking?" Who is this person with the question, and what is her agenda? The person raising the question is but one of many on an interviewing committee. Each interviewer will come at you from a different perspective, perhaps with a different end game in mind. Knowing who and how they operate is valuable information. Understanding the makeup of the committee, how it was formed, what prejudices members may hold, the diversity of views it possesses, and the mission it was given are essential data for the candidate.

No job-hunt guide would be complete without a comprehensive look at interviewing committees. Regardless of what position is being filled by a school district, there invariably will be one or more interviewing committees in place. The makeup of committees should always reflect the philosophical attitude of the superintendent and the governing board; therefore, you can expect that every district will have a somewhat individualized format. Nevertheless, within these personalized formats, there are common threads that weave themselves through all school systems and that are reflected in interviewing committees.

INTERVIEWING COMMITTEES IN GENERAL

Understanding who serves on committees is important to the candidate since he needs to tailor responses for different audiences. This does not mean you play to an audience, but it does require that you provide information that is sought by each committee. The most difficult committee for a candidate to deal with is a mixed committee, a committee made up of representatives of the many constituencies in education. The difficulty arises because each member often is waiting for a response that others do not seek. This is compounded by the fact that in education, unlike most other professions, interviewing committees often include individuals from outside the profession. For example, a committee interviewing a superintendent candidate often has representatives from civic organizations, political entities, town employees, parent groups, minority organizations, senior citizens groups, and others. Consider the potential conflict for the candidate when parents want greater expenditures for education while representatives from any one of the other groups may be seeking a cap on the tax rate. Principals may desire a strong leader, while a governing board may want someone who can be micromanaged.

Even within the professional staff there are potential conflicts. For example, teachers and parents may not agree on student grouping practices or on how teacher planning time should be utilized. Parents may seek a principal who can "clean house," while the staff likes things as they are.

INTERVIEWING COMMITTEES ORGANIZED BY POSITION

There was a time in the distant past when principals hired teachers, superintendents hired administrators, and governing boards hired superintendents. This was accomplished without the inclusion of other parties. Over the past twenty-five years or so, there has been a steady change in the hiring process such that almost every position is filled by a committee with a diverse membership. While the administrator in charge of a search may favor one candidate over another, it would be difficult not to follow the recommendation of the interviewing committee. An administrator who ignores such a recommendation often does so at her own peril. Because of the immense leverage a committee has, a candidate must understand the makeup of the committee and know how to deal with the diverse membership.

Teacher Interviewing Committees

If you are a teacher candidate being interviewed by a committee, it will generally be comprised of the building administrator or department chair, other teachers from your grade or department, and parents. Usually a representative from the nonclassroom staff, such as guidance, will be included. You will have arrived at this stage in the process after your application and other materials were reviewed at the building or department level. As a result of that review, you appeared to be a qualified candidate. Possibly you had a screening interview prior to the committee interview; that will vary by district. Now you are at the final stage of the competition. Depending upon the size of the district, a personnel director or other central office administrator might be present, representing the superintendent's interest.

As innocent as the committee makeup appears, it represents many varying interests. The teachers on the committee are usually the most outspoken in the school. That generally is how they get to serve! They may want a pliable recruit, while the principal may want a strong individual. The grade level you would be assigned to may have had low test scores for several years, and the superintendent may want a teacher who can bring academic rigor, while the other teachers may be content with things as they are. The point is that an innocuous looking committee will always have diverse opinions about what is sought in the new staff member. You need to be careful that the positions you take are not so hard and fast that you cannot appeal to most of the committee members. The best advice offered is that you must always come down on the moral and ethical side of an issue that best serves students. In the final analysis, only students comprise your constituency.

Administrator Interview Committees

Because of the wide range of administrative positions in a district, the composition of interviewing committees will vary. However, there are similar components to all of them. You can be certain that there will be representatives from the administrative organization, teacher association, parent groups, and central office. Depending upon the position to be filled, districts may include representatives from the support staff, such as instructional aides and secretarial/clerical staff. Many superintendents now include a governing board member on administrator interviewing committees. The superintendent usually participates.

The same concerns noted for a teacher interview committee carry over to this committee. Because of the even greater diversity of the membership, an administrator has a more difficult time attempting to address all views while not deserting his principles. I think it is obvious that not all members of the committee will value the same qualities in the candidates.

In an earlier chapter, the point was made that there times when a parent who has a problem at the classroom or building level may need to have the problem addressed, not at the bottom of the hierarchy, but somewhere above that, perhaps even at the superintendent level. For example, a parent may have had a very difficult time with a classroom teacher with another child and feels threatened to deal with her in regard to a child now assigned to the same teacher. Or the parent may have had a dispute with the principal over another matter and has reason to believe she will not be treated fairly now. There are multiple reasons why starting other than at the bottom of the hierarchy to solve a problem makes sense.

Therefore, a look at the makeup of the typical administrator interview committee makes it clear that there will be diverse and potentially controversial views on the issue as to where in the hierarchy a problem-solving effort should begin. Clearly, principals and teachers on an interviewing committee will look at this issue in a way different from that of a superintendent or parent on the committee. Other issues that will not have a single philosophy among the interviewers include student discipline, comprehensive annual testing, homogeneous versus heterogeneous grouping, class rank calculation, athletic team-cutting policy, selection process for valedictorian, dealing with an inferior teacher, and many others.

The best advice offered is to think before you speak, believe in what you say, and say it with conviction. You represent students, not adults. Although you are expected to be a partner, you are required to be a leader. Where do you wish to be positioned on the administrator ability continuum? Do you want to hunker down safely in the middle of the continuum, or do you want to join the ranks of the courageous administrators who believe in doing what is right? The choice is always yours.

Superintendent Interview Committees

Very recently, a few governing boards have reverted to the old style of recruiting a superintendent by excluding other parties from the process. Superintendent candidates find this the best of all worlds because their names are not made public until the very end of the process. There is no aspect of a job hunt that is more unsettling to a superintendent candidate, especially an experienced one, than that of having his name in the public arena early in the process. Any action that a hiring district can take to avoid early disclosure will result in many more experienced candidates applying. The perception in your home community is that if you come in second in your job hunt in another community, it is like coming in last. You lose a little of your glitter back home.

However, the process described above is the exception. A superintendent search process remains one of the most complicated of all job-hunt procedures employed by a governing board or its agents. The interview process usually involves more than one committee. The general practice is for a governing board to act as one interviewing group, and for a more diverse group to be engaged as a second interview committee. The diverse committee makeup will vary from district to district, but it is a fact that most segments of the community will be involved either directly or through representatives. It will be somewhat different from a committee established for a principal search because the superintendent committee will involve more individuals from civic, political, and community groups, including nonprofit agencies that interact with the schools.

Although superintendent candidates usually are more comfortable with interviewing committees than teachers and administrators, they need to exert caution in how they respond to questions. As noted earlier, members on a diverse committee will have different expectations. For, example, the average citizen group is comprised of many subcultures. You have parents with children in school and parents with children yet to enter school. Seniors are comprised of adults without children, empty nesters whose kids are out of school, and older seniors with younger spouses with children still in school. It is safe to say that each group will have a different view on what the appropriate expenditure level should be for the school district. This is only one example of diversity. The same can be said for every group represented on the committee. The areas of potential conflict are many.

ONCE AGAIN, "WHO'S ASKING"

Whether you are a competing for a teacher or administrator position, the makeup of the interviewing committee is vitally important. While the person asking you the question is, at that moment, the most important person on the committee, each of the others has a keen interest in your response. They will be comparing your responses to the standard they have established in their own minds. The representative from the local youth service agency has expectations for the schools that differ from the athletic department. The law enforcement agency has views on discipline decidedly different from those of most principals. Representative from town government have ideas for the use of tax dollars that differ from those of the school department. On and on it goes, with each representative group posing different questions and expecting different responses. It is obvious that there will never be consensus among the group regarding the answers you provide to their questions. The diversity of thought around the table makes consensus impossible. Your answers will never satisfy all interviewers.

FINALLY, THE CORRECT ANSWER

What, then, are the appropriate answers to their questions? The solution to the dilemma posed is quite simple but requires courage. As a candidate you must rally the interviewers—but not around your responses for the obvious reasons noted above; rather, you must rally them around you! One personal example in this guide will help make this point.

For twenty-five years, a resident of my town came to most of my budget meetings, at which time he would flail away at my school budget. During those years he also had lodged a number of grievances with my athletic department. He had a rather contentious relationship with the school system. The year in which I retired, I took up golf at the same club at which he was a member. Knowing nothing about golf, I would stop at the course on the way home from work during my last year as superintendent and try hitting a few balls. One day I was on the driving range armed only with a single used seven iron. I was in my dress clothes and wore dress shoes. Next to me on the range was the gentleman noted above. He turned and asked me where my clubs were. I told him that I was a new member and had yet to buy clubs. At which point he said, "Use mine."

I did so and said, "Thank you." It is important to note that his clubs were brand new and obviously expensive.

Shortly hereafter he asked, "Where's your glove?"

I answered, "I don't have one."

He said, "I have an extra one you are welcome to use."

I accepted his offer. Then he offered a few suggestions on how to swing the club. Within a few weeks, he invited me to play golf with him.

The important lesson to be learned is that in all those years when he opposed my budget and had difficulty with the policies of my athletic department, he never opposed me! He knew what I stood for and respected it even if he did not agree with my stance on an issue. The strength of my conviction was meaningful to him. I treated him with respect, never expecting anything in return, and he, in turn, respected the commitment I had to students. To this day, thirty-five years later, he is the consummate gentleman to me and to my wife.

If you want to earn the respect of an interviewing committee, you need to be you. Your answers must reflect what you believe. You can never forget that your only commitment is to the clients; in this case, the clients of every educator are the young children, the adolescents, and the young adults in your care. If you are unsure what it is you need to say to the interviewers, then take a deep breath, a fictitious drag on cigarette (much like the Perry Mason character), and remember that you are answering on behalf of children. You cannot go wrong.

16

SPECIAL THOUGHTS FOR ASPIRING TEACHERS

In chapter 1, "Avoid the Art of Failure," I mentioned that during my career as a superintendent of schools, I hired approximately 500 educators, the vast majority of them being teachers, both inexperienced and experienced. Because of the relatively small size of the district I ran at that time, I did not have a human relations department; therefore, I was involved in the hiring of every educator. The system I employed then is still the model in most small systems, and small systems still constitute the majority of school districts in the nation.

This chapter is designed specifically for those about to job hunt for their first teaching position, the first rung on the educational career ladder. Although procedures vary from district to district, there are similar themes in all job searches.

As you review this chapter, keep in mind that all of the information provided in this guide also pertains to teacher candidates seeking their first position in education. While the position you seek is on the first rung of the professional educator career ladder, districts seek the same qualities in you that they seek in all other professionals. The difference is that you have little or no experience in the job-hunt process. Almost everything is new and challenging. Consequently, you need more guidance than experienced candidates do during the job-hunt process. This guide will be of enormous help to you.

Although the vast majority of candidates seeking their first teaching position will be graduates of schools of education, there is another small percentage of professionals who are coming to the job hunt from alternative routes. Many states now have programs that provide an opportunity for those who work in the private sector, and who have special talents, to acquire teaching certification in a shorter period of time through an alternative program. For them, the job hunt is more difficult because they generally have little understanding of the educational culture and because not all school systems view these candidates as being of the same caliber as those who graduate from schools of education. Regardless of the route by which you enter education, this guide provides a valuable resource.

HOW A SEARCH BEGINS FOR BEGINNERS

Usually, applications are logged into the system and generally codified by grade and subject matter taught. Department heads and principals usually review applications and select those that meet certain district-established criteria. Interviewing takes place at either the department or building level, depending upon the time of year and the personal preference of principals.

Once the initial screening interviews are completed, a principal, in conjunction with a department chair, will identify the most qualified. If a screening committee is utilized, the candidates will move on to be interviewed by that committee. Chapter 15 discusses the makeup of such a committee and the motives that the diverse membership may possess. Teacher candidates should review that chapter. Chapter 18 provides advice as to the best time of year to engage in a job hunt if you are unsuccessful during the regular December to May recruiting window.

An alternative selection process is for a principal, after preliminary decisions are made at the department and building levels, to recommend two to four candidates to the superintendent for his consideration. This is my personal preference since if I, as superintendent, am responsible for the success of the system, I need to both employ and deploy human resources as I deem fit after consultation with appropriate administrators.

In a large system, an assistant superintendent or deputy superintendent will usually fulfill the role of superintendent in the hiring process. In so doing, he will use as a guideline the hiring philosophy of the superintendent. Whatever system is utilized, the same basic philosophy is at work. There will be exceptions to the traditional recruiting process described above when there is an acute shortage of teachers. In this case, a district may be compelled to forgo one or more of the steps in a typical process. Occasionally, a candidate will be hired without a thorough background check or review of credentials. If you are involved in such a recruiting process, you are well advised to review carefully chapter 2, "The Career Ladder."

Having personally interviewed over 2,000 candidates to fill approximately 500 teaching positions over a twenty-five-year period, I believe that I can offer advice to aspiring teachers. The suggestions made throughout this guide for educators in general and for those wishing to change careers and move into education are valuable for aspiring teachers, and I have some additional suggestions that are also appropriate.

You may recall that chapter 4 addresses the site visit and background checks that should be made before any candidate is hired. Rarely is a site visit conducted for a teacher candidate. Most often, the background check will be conducted by phone or by personal contact with one or more of a candidate's college supervisors, student teacher advisors, mentor teachers, or building administrators with whom the teacher has worked.

FIVE STANDARDS

What is the district seeking in a new teacher? Assume for a moment that there is evidence that the candidate has had successful student teacher experience and that there is nothing in her personal or professional life to bring instability to the hiring. What else is important? Given the thousands of school districts in the nation, obviously there will be differences in priorities, but there are some aspects that thread their way through all hiring processes. They are timeless because they deal with the human character, not with data.

For twenty-five years, I used the same rating scale to seek the "other" qualities I believed important in candidates for all teaching and administrative positions. These are qualities in addition to those you have read throughout this guide.

First, I assess the degree to which I believe a candidate will be able to handle crises immediately. Education is a profession in which crisis lurks around each corner. Whether it is an accident on the playground, a life-threatening food allergy emergency, a young child missing from school, students harassing one another, or an abusive student, a teacher needs the skills to respond appropriately and effectively.

Second, I need evidence of a candidate's management ability. While we accept as a matter of fact that administrators need to possess outstanding management skills, we often fail to recognize that the modern teacher assignment is filled with management demands. Good management skills are required when handling test score data, student assignments, attendance records, and general classroom activities. The paper burden on teachers has grown each year.

Third, I want evidence of a candidate's high level of effective interpersonal skills. Education is a people business and a teacher needs to possess the ability to interact effectively and responsibly with students, parents, staff, and administration. Many teachers with outstanding academic records and classroom successes have failed because of an inability to interact with other adults.

Fourth, I am interested in a candidate's poise, carriage, and the messages they send. Nonverbal messages are as powerful as verbal and written ones. The way one carries oneself will project to others an image of confidence or insecurity. Before you even utter your first word when meeting parents, they will quickly, for better or worse, make a judgment about you based on your body language.

Fifth, I look for a candidate who has potential for growth. No school system will be satisfied with what a new teacher learned during the undergraduate or student teacher experiences. Those alone will not be adequate for the long-term demands of the classroom. Therefore, the candidate must possess the will and ability to continue with his formal education and to be an active participant in local professional development activities. Every new teacher should have the potential to become a mentor to others.

The five standards listed above are important to many hiring agents. They help employers distinguish the candidates from one another and to assist them in making final judgements. But the standards are also of value to the candidates. While such standards are not similar in all districts, they are sufficiently common to provide you with a yardstick. You need to think in terms of how you compare with the standards.

Last, the higher the expectation of a district, the more likely it is the place you want to work. When an employer's primary goal is to fill a vacancy rather than hire the best, you should look elsewhere for work. Outstanding districts seek outstanding recruits. You have the task of assessing the district to determine if it is the place where you want to begin your career.

17

LIFE AT THE TOP: THE UNIVERSE OF SUPERINTENDENTS

What is interesting about the superintendent position is that there is no truly effective way to train for it. Many models have been tried but none realistically reflect what the job entails because no model can place you in a situation that accurately mirrors all aspects of the position. We place pilots into training simulators but we have no such sophisticated tool for those leading a school system or business. Administrators often believe that if they are successful in the professional positions immediately below that of superintendent, they will therefore be successful at the top of the hierarchy. Unfortunately, this is flawed thinking. The responsibilities of the superintendent position are light years away from the limited responsibilities of other positions, including that of deputy superintendent.

It is not the intent in this chapter to describe the work of a superintendent except to the extent that the position is at the pinnacle of the elementary and secondary school hierarchy. For many years, there has been an acute shortage of qualified educators to fill the position of superintendent of schools. As of this writing, the shortage is more pronounced than it has been at any time in modern U.S. history. Consequently, it is understandable that a percentage of those who are appointed to the position are, at best, marginal in terms of ability.

Superintendents constitute a universe of their own, much like lawyers, doctors, CEOs, and accountants, all of whom operate in their separate universes. And, like those in other professions, superintendents spread out over a bell curve in terms of ability. Every profession hopes that the bell curve that depicts it is skewed to the higher ability side. I have no doubt that superintendents are more talented than most professionals in other management fields. My experience in having worked with them both as a colleague and as a consultant validates my belief that superintendents are a unique breed of men and women who care deeply about children and who work for noble causes.

In the middle of the bell curve are the majority of superintendents, men and women of steady habits, highly skilled, good at what they do, and who always seem do what needs to be done. As a group, they are caring about children and supportive of qualified staff. They don't often make mistakes. They make every effort to rid the profession of marginal and incompetent employees. They provide the undergirding of the elementary and secondary public school systems in the nation. On one hand, they do not, as a rule, get districts in trouble and, on the other hand, they do not always bring star quality to a district. They are educational leaders who represent most districts in the country. They are not usually at serious risk because they are not defined as risk takers. They are what make public education work. Without them at the helm, there would be no effective U.S. public school system.

At one end of the curve, there is a small group of exceptionally talented and outstanding men and women who are defined as agents of change and improvement. They are risk takers who have a vision for schools that others in education don't always embrace. These educators tend to be courageous and willing to risk their livelihoods to promote what they believe are important initiatives. No challenge is insurmountable. What they do is often controversial. They are willing to endure personal sacrifices in order to push for change. Without them, many of the programs employed in public education would not exist. As a young teacher, I worked in a district for just such a superintendent, and it was exhilarating to watch him lead and to observe his courage in risking a career to promote quality initiatives. His enthusiasm was contagious.

At the other end of the bell curve are those who are marginally competent or not competent. In either case, they are the products of the acute shortage of qualified administrators, ineffective recruiting by a governing board, or appointed through pure political patronage. These superintendents are destructive to the process of quality education. Often it is not until they have done considerable damage that they are ousted. In the meantime, countless students have been denied a quality educational experience.

LIVING AT THE TOP

The position of superintendent is significantly different from all other administrative jobs in elementary and secondary public education. The professional move to this position entails a major change in lifestyle. No matter where you are or when you are there, your life belongs to the district. You cannot avoid crises, hide from tough decisions, or escape the demanding pace of the position. Successes belong to others; setbacks are yours alone. Essentially, you are a prisoner of your profession. The public nature of it is unlike most other professional positions in the nation. Your smallest blemish is exposed, your family will be subject to public scrutiny, and your personal habits are the stuff that gossip is made from.

It should be obvious that before you make the decision to compete for the position of superintendent of schools, you must engage in outstanding research and use every element of your personal and professional networks to find answers to the many questions you must raise.

This chapter was written for a specific reason. Through the years, I have known of and worked with administrators who wanted a position of greater responsibility. No matter what position you currently hold in education, the move to the next step in the hierarchy holds out both opportunities and risks. These risks increase as you move from a staff position to a line position. The risks increase exponentially as you move up the line position hierarchy, with each step increasing public exposure and scrutiny of your professional and personal life.

It was pointed out that principals at all grade levels have difficult assignments. Many burn out at some point in their career and look to other opportunities. Some look to a central office position. When a principal enters a central office environment, it is much like an aircraft reaching its cruising altitude. If he pays attention to the flight plan, there is limited danger and only a small degree of risk. It is when there is a change in the flight plan and a decision is made to move higher and travel faster that the risks begin to take quantum leaps. Once one enters the superintendent's domain, there is an immediate and powerful set of conditions to contend with, many of which portend professional risk unless caution is exerted.

The Double-Edged Sword of the Media

Until an educator becomes a superintendent of schools, she is somewhat immune from the two greatest risk factors in education: the media and the governing board. Both are capable of wielding menacing swords. While principals have some exposure to the media and a governing board, they also have the superintendent to assist them when problems arise or to take over a controversial issue that occurred at the building level.

There is little a superintendent can do as it relates to the media. Reporters and correspondents who work for newspapers, radio, and TV have but one allegiance, and it is to their organizations. They have sole possession of the megaphones! Unless the media decides otherwise, your comments will always be defensive ones. The media has its own universe, and its reporters and correspondents also spread out on a "competency" bell curve. Although the media leadership would have us believe that all of those employed by them are outstanding or at least above average, personal experience tells me otherwise. I have had experience with newspaper reporters who were negative in outlook, and most of what they wrote reflected this attitude. Others went about their work on a more positive note. But the bottom line is that a superintendent is naive to think he can influence what is to be written, spoken, or shown, either about him personally or about his district. Media reporters are mainly interested in the story line and what is defined as news: the timely, unique, sordid, or controversial. My advice is to develop a professional relationship with local media and stick only to the facts.

Before accepting a superintendent position, you need to recognize the risks involved in certain situations and communities and decide if you want to deal with them. For example, if you take a position in a district that has local talk radio, you will probably experience some uncomfortable times. I conducted a search in a small city with a locally owned talk show, and it frequently criticized the school system. The superintendent and board then had to counter the negative messages that emanated from the talk show. A colleague of mine worked as a superintendent in a community with talk radio and, until it went off the air, he fought a constant battle to correct the show's misinformation or to counter it. To some talk radio programs, accuracy can be unimportant.

One of the best ways for the media to increase circulation or expand a listening audience is to "take on" public officials. There are some districts that are covered by a newspaper that is generally recognized as not being particularly sympathetic towards public administrators. You might want to avoid working in a district that has this quality of coverage. No matter where you work, however, there will be media attention of some kind. Assessing its objectivity is one way to help determine if you wish to work in a particular district.

Machiavellian Outlook

The second most serious threat to a superintendent's career is the governing board. A governing board is a peculiar entity. In the vast majority of communities in the country, anyone can serve. There are no requirements to govern, and a board's agenda is whatever it wants it to be. Most communities have to exert a major effort to find citizens to run for office. Once a citizen is appointed to a governing board, she can remain for many years in most districts. The use of executive session affords a way for a board to avoid public scrutiny on issues that are often of public interest. While the law is narrow in what can be discussed in executive session, a board has broad leeway in what it discusses off the record. Boards that meet for dinner or at an informal get-together prior to the official meeting have an opportunity, outside of the public eye, to reach agreements that should have been aired in public. Unless a superintendent has a contractual agreement with the board that he or a designee maintains the right to be present at every meeting of the board, without exception, there are opportunities for a board to have a private discussion the results of which can undermine a superintendent.

Depending upon who is serving at a given time, you could be working for a governing board trained in Machiavellian tactics, or you could be associated with men and women whose respect for others is the basis for governing. Both types of boards exist; I have worked for both in my several roles as interim superintendent. Unlike the media, over which you have little control, as an aspiring or experienced superintendent, you do have total control over your own position with the governing board issue: you need not work for it! Once again, you must implement the job-search mantra: "research, research, and research!"

Thankfully for superintendent candidates, governing boards and individual board members leave their fingerprints everywhere. The Internet has eased considerably the research aspect of a job search. And, if Holmes and Watson were in the neighborhood, they would advise you where to look. A good place to start is the local district website where you can review board minutes. If the minutes have been accurately recorded, they will provide a candidate with a relatively clear understanding of a board's values.

You also learn which of the members play powerful roles in steering decisions and in creating district culture. Every board has an informal leader, sometimes more, who often controls or influences the actions of the formal chair through his ability to stymie action on agenda items or to muscle through items for vested interests. Others on the board may be connected to other powerful persons in the community, some of whom serve on other boards whose actions often impact the activities of the governing board. An examination of the work of board committees tells you a great deal about the relative influence of its members. The committees to which governing board members are assigned by the chairperson will speak volumes about the relative importance and power of individual members.

The most effective tool for uncovering the fingerprints of a governing board or of individual board members is through professional networking. There are communities that have a reputation for being difficult with superintendents. There are boards that are committed to micromanaging. Still other boards have a history of being disrespectful and abusive of educators. While the membership may change from election to election, the culture of a board might not change, depending upon the personalities. However, there are boards and communities that have long histories of being outstanding. I am among the very fortunate in that I worked as superintendent for twenty-five years in a community in which all boards over that period were exceptional. But in my role as consultant and interim superintendent, I have worked with boards of all types, some as good as they get and others as bad as they get.

The lesson for superintendent candidates is that before committing to a new position, be certain that you have realistically assessed your chance of success in a community if a board has values that are incompatible with your own. The time to cut your loses is before you commit to the district.

As stated in chapter 2, don't rush in where angels fear to tread!

REFLECTIONS

It would be fabulous if a candidate could cross the finish line in first place the first time out of the gate. While that is not always possible, I know of many candidates who did just that. They walked into their first interview on one step of their career ladder and walked out on another, higher step of the ladder. They managed to be successful primarily because they conducted the research needed to collect background data and found sources of information that assisted them throughout the preparation for and the completion of a perfect job hunt. Many of these candidates and their stories are noted throughout this guide.

THANK THE HELPERS

For those who experienced early success in the job quest, there is little for them to do except to reflect on their experience and extend thanks to the many professionals who assisted them and who made it possible for them to grow and mature in their jobs. They need to be sufficiently humble to recognize that even the most talented professionals rarely make it on their own. So often we forget to extend appreciation to those who helped us exceed our own expectations. One way for you to begin the process of creating an effective network is to take the time now to thank those who helped you get to your current position. They are also the ones you may need in the future.

CALLBACKS

If you came in second, there is an important and uplifting thought to bear in mind. The uplifting aspect is what is referred to as a "callback." It is not unusual to come in second in your quest for a specific position in a district only to be called back at a later date for another opening in the district, even though it may be a different job. Someone who was part of the first search you participated in saw qualities in you that were sufficiently impressive to make a callback. This action occurs with frequency and especially in a tight job market. My first superintendent search contract was the result of a callback. I didn't get the consulting job I interviewed for my first time out, but someone on that governing board was sufficiently impressed to ask my firm to conduct an executive search for another position. Important events do turn on small hinges!

Not only did I make those callbacks when I was superintendent, but as a consultant I have worked with a number of candidates who have had a callback experience. Clients often ask about a candidate who was not hired but who was nevertheless considered a quality individual. It is important to remember that the makeup of the pool of candidates shifts on a daily basis and someone who was not chosen on April 4th because of the strength of the pool at that time may be considered competitive the following July 17th. If you are not competitive this year, you may be competitive next year.

Large urban districts, in particular, almost always have two or more positions that are similar, such as elementary school principals, and will make a callback to a candidate who was not offered the first opening but who was considered a strong candidate for the second elementary school opening. If you were not hired the first time you interviewed, do not publicly complain about the district. Don't burn your bridges. You may need to cross one or more of them to get to your second chance in the district!

The remainder of this final chapter is not written for those candidates who made it to the winner's circle the first time out, nor for those who received a callback. It is written for those who do not come in first and who did not receive a callback. One of the early thoughts expressed in the first chapter of this book was that coming in second is no better than coming in last. Although some candidates may deem being second acceptable, it is those who refuse to be second the next time out who will eventually prevail in a job search. Being second is not being a failure—if you learn from the experience. Reflecting on what occurred is vital to the recycling process and another run for the ribbon.

DEBRIEFING BEGINS

Chapter 1 raised several questions that need repeating now. You have to ask yourself:

- Why is it that some candidates are hired and others are continually passed over?
- What is the secret of getting employment when you have the professional credentials that often are superior to those of the candidate selected?
- What mistakes did you make early in the application process that resulted in your not being moved along?
- Why is it that after only a few minutes into an interview you know you are out of the running?
- Or, why after what you thought was a great interview, were you not offered the position?
- What words or phrases turned interviewers off?
- What interviewing strategies did you fail to employ?
- How well prepared were you for the interview?
- At what point in the interview did you lose your advantage?
- What caused interviewers to fail to recognize your talents?
- What mannerisms did you display that embarrassed interviewers?
- What really went wrong, and why hasn't anyone told you?
- What impressions did you create with your opening comments and concluding remarks?

Reflecting openly upon these questions will be a good start to your debriefing efforts. Since the interview is the last of all the job-search activities a candidate engages in, it should be the first activity to be reviewed since it is the freshest in his mind.

There are important questions you need to ask because they pertain to your perceptions as to what occurred during the interview process.

What went well? Review the interview from the moment you met the chair to the time you shook her hand on the way out of the door and list the positives.

What didn't go so well? Use the same process as in the first question.

What will you do differently next time? This list should be comprised of the positive aspects you would reinforce and the negative aspects you would change and how you would change them.

While acquiring accurate information from the chair of the interviewing committee or from individual interviewers would be valuable, the chances of acquiring it are minimal. The worry that a candidate might initiate litigation discourages a district from providing any feedback except that which is of little value. If a consultant is involved in the process, he could be a valuable source of feedback, but that only works if the consultant is present at the interview.

Debriefing Pitfall

Candidates who attempt to debrief themselves usually have little trouble reflecting upon the question-and-answer elements of the interview. They will be forthright with themselves in noting a good response from poor one, which question they ran with, and which question derailed them. It is when they have to reflect on their personal qualities that they are unrealistic. No one wants to rate themselves poorly on interpersonal skills and personal qualities. As a superintendent of schools, one of the most difficult situations to be in is to advise an employee on personal matters. It is a significantly more delicate issue than dealing with employee disciplinary matters. It is the strongest argument yet as to why private job coaching is so valuable. An objective third party is paid to be forthright with the candidate when it comes to discussing personal matters and personality issues.

Revisit This Guide

Once the interview has been thoroughly analyzed, then it is time to revisit chapters 1 and 8, which are basically alerts as to what can go wrong in a search and raise questions that have to be answered before you venture out once again. At this stage, you have learned a great deal about yourself as a result of the preparation for the job search and from the give-and-take at the interview. You have a much better chance to see yourself as others do. It is an opportunity to raise fundamental questions the answers to which will better prepare you for your next attempt.

A job hunt is a stressful and time-consuming process. It is easy to become discouraged. There are moments when you begin to question yourself and wonder if you should stay where you are and ride it out to retirement. Many candidates do just that because there is a certain degree of embarrassment as you share with others the discouraging news about your unsuccessful search. You need to be strong of character to keep at it when it would be so easy to stop your quest, to end the job hunt. It is a moment of truth for many.

RETURNING TO THE STARTING GATE

Having made up your mind that you have the heart and the talent to stay the course, you need to initiate another job hunt. Assume for a moment that the normal recruiting season is over and that schools have shut down for the summer vacation. For you, there is no vacation! Although the primary recruiting period has ended, there will always be additional openings occurring all year long. This is especially true during the summer months and shortly after school has started in the fall. Unexpected illnesses, spousal transfers, maternity and other leaves, and increases in enrollments will require new additions to the staff in almost every district in the nation. The larger the district, the more likely there will be an opening in your area of expertise. Therefore, it makes sense for you to get back to the starting gate.

Because the summer months present the best opportunity to be hired if you were unsuccessful in the spring, there is a need to be prepared. How do you prepare for jobs that have yet to be announced?

1. Determine the commuting distance you are willing to travel. How far will depend upon many factors, including how badly you need employment.
2. Keep in touch with districts within the commuting distance on a weekly basis to learn of job openings.
3. Prepare a complete recruiting package and be ready to send it to a district on a moment's notice. The package should include an up-to-date cover letter and resume, three current and dated letters of reference, and the names and addresses of three other references who may be contacted by a school system interested in you.
4. Include a copy of your certification since it is an important piece of information. A certified candidate has a much better chance of being employed late in the summer or at the last minute than one who has yet to apply for certification.
5. Make certain that you inform the potential employer how to contact you easily during the summer months.

The five suggestions above are based on the fact that classrooms need to be staffed by school opening at the beginning of the school year. School districts would prefer to avoid using long-term substitutes when opening schools. Parents want permanent teachers and administrators in place. Therefore, a district will make every effort to hire competent candidates. Because time is short and gets shorter as the summer months unfold, candidates who have all of their papers in order will have the best opportunity to be hired. July and August provide candidates with a unique opportunity to complete a successful job hunt.

IT BEGINS AND ENDS WITH BELIEF IN SELF

I end this guide where I began it. It was my nineteenth interview that spelled my success and that opened a long, successful, and wonderful career that has spanned more than thirty-five years. There were eighteen opportunities when I could have called it quits, but I did not quit because I believed in myself. Importantly, my first principal believed in me and provided some tough but valuable advice about how to move my career along. It would have been so much easier to stay put because I worked in a great school and lived in a wonderful community, but I believed that I could bring some value to educational leadership. You, too, must believe in your leadership ability. Only you can create the will to persevere. If you are determined to lead, you will undoubtedly do so.

EPILOGUE

The warriors, braves, and elders had left; silence enveloped the village. Silhouetted against the sky were two lonely figures, the last of many who had assembled at sunrise at the chief's request. The smaller and older of the two was slightly stooped yet left the impression of regal strength. The other was tall and lean, young, with a bearing that spoke to his confident nature.

The sun was setting, with a sliver already settled below the horizon. In a few minutes darkness would settle in. It had been a long and arduous day for the chief, a day in which all of those assembled, with one exception, left the village disappointed, and a day that sealed the fate of his tribe for many years.

The younger man broke the silence. "Why, from among the bravest, most experienced, and proven warriors, did you select me to follow in your footsteps? I do not compare with the most daring among the warriors, I am not the strongest nor fastest of the braves. I do not possess the wisdom of the elders. I am young, and while strong of body and mind, have not experienced the events of the past. Traditions have not yet touched my soul, and I have made no sacrifices for the people. Unlike your son, I am from a family without history, and I have not traveled far from this village. My schooling is but from my mother, and my skills of hunting and survival from none other than my father, an honorable man but a man without distinction among the village elders. While I see the horizon each day, I have but a few times traveled beyond it. I am only of this village. Why me?"

The chief had anticipated that the moment would come when the young brave would need to be told why he had been chosen, told things about himself that he did not yet understand.

"I care not where you come from, I care only who you are. I worry not about your being fleet of foot, I seek a swiftness of thought. Your schooling is important, not because of who taught you, but what they taught you. It is not how far you have traveled, but with whom you traveled and what you learned in your travels. Some in our village measure bravery by the accuracy of the arrow, but the time is right to measure bravery by who is able to secure the future of our people. Rushing to a victory over an enemy pales before walking calmly to the place of wisdom."

"How do you know that I possess the qualities you describe?"

"I know that your parents instilled in you the kindness and integrity that all leaders must possess, yet qualities that escape so many of those entrusted with the fate of others. Your parents taught you the value of working together as a family to protect what you have earned and to secure the future, a lesson that many chiefs in this nation have yet to learn. Although your parents did not travel far afoot, they reached out to many for the wisdom they shared with you and that so often is lacking in those who lead. You have learned from those in this village that while traditions and customs must be honored, survival and growth will demand you cut new trails, forge new alliances, and embrace creative ideas. You have come to know, by observing your elders, that it is from others that leadership is nurtured, and therefore it must be shared with others. The strongest of leaders are those who listen to others. You have seen these things in the way that the elders share their thoughts with one another and me. Each of us in our own way has taught you that bravery with ideas is mightier than the strength of your hand. But the most important lesson of all is to believe that although others can teach you the mechanics of *how* to decide, only your values determine *what* you decide. What you come to believe is not what others want you to believe, it is what you know is right for the people. I look for you to remember all of these lessons, lessons lost to most leaders."

The young brave spoke, "You are the wisest of us all. Share with me what you believe will be the greatest challenge I shall face when tomorrow comes."

The chief thought for a moment and then shared his wisdom with the new chief. "There is but one village but there are many voices within it. The elders, although concerned about the future of the tribe, will see the past as the blueprint for the days ahead. It is natural because their years are limited, and they need the security that comes with remembering the past. They have earned their rest. The warriors, who command respect of many because of their proven heroism, will be restless with a new chief. In the beginning they will not speak out because of their respect for me, but sooner or later they will challenge you. For them the future is now. The only battle they wish to fight will be with the new leadership. The braves, many of whom are your friends since childhood, will support you for they will see such support as defending youth and its new ideas. For them the future is bright but still ill defined. Remember, however, that many among them desired to be the new chief. Finally, you have the women. You must not underestimate their influence upon everyone in the village. Because they speak for the children of this generation and of the next generation, they, more than all others, will speak more eloquently and powerfully for what is right and just. They may be the strongest of your allies."

"How do I balance the interests of so many?"

"If you lead, you will be challenged. It is in the nature of Man not to be accepting of the ideas of others. From the challenges will come new ideas and opportunities to improve the lives of those in the village. No matter how badly others behave, maintain your ideals. No matter how abusive their language, maintain the morality of your position. No matter how threatening others may be, use integrity as your defense. One day you will find that all in this village will understand and appreciate the strength of your character and your focus on the needs of others. At that point, they will continue to challenge your ideas, but they will not challenge you! When that moment comes, you will finally be chief."

As the final moment of daylight was slipping below the horizon, the chief spoke his final words. "When the sun rises in the morning, you will lead this tribe. When that day comes when you pass your authority to yet another chief, you will be judged, as I have been, by what you have accomplished for the benefit of others."

ABOUT THE AUTHOR

Herbert F. Pandiscio was superintendent of schools in Avon, Connecticut, for twenty-five years before taking an early retirement. Shortly thereafter, he formed Herbert William Consulting Inc., an administrative search firm specializing in identifying and hiring school superintendents, central office employees, and school administrators. He brings credibility to the many suggestions and ideas offered in this guide through his experience of having served as a teacher, coach, assistant principal, principal, assistant superintendent, and superintendent of schools. This was followed by more than ten years as a search consultant, private job-coaching specialist, and interim superintendent in numerous districts.

The author has personally interviewed and hired hundreds of employees for public schools and nonprofit organizations. He has reviewed thousands of applications received from aspiring administrators, experienced administrators seeking new positions, and teacher candidates. Throughout the years, he has documented the best and worst of candidates' job-search efforts. This guide is a story of those successes and failures. It is a roadmap for a successful job hunt.